"Melinda Ribner has written an exceptional book—intriguing and elucidating. *New Age Judaism* delineates the true and ancient wisdom of the Torah and of Judaism in the context of its interrelationship with many of the precepts of New Age conceptualization. Ms. Ribner's knowledge of philosophical and metaphysical Judaism is extensive. She presents this knowledge in a sensitive and enthusiastic manner. This book should be considered a relevant and novel addition for many a library and collector and should be especially useful to individuals interested in the world of theology and philosophy."

—**Rabbi Mordecai Tendler**
Yeshiva University

"Melinda Ribner is an accomplished *mashpiya* (spiritual guide and transmitter). She guides contemporary people by offering them tools to experience God and Judaism firsthand. In her *New Age Judaism,* she shows you an affordable and accessible path to your soul."

—**Rabbi Zalman Schachter-Shalomi**
Aleph, Alliance for Jewish Renewal

"A wonderful account of New Age Judaism that is chock full of practical skills from a most sincere, spiritual traveler."

—**Rabbi Shoni Labowitz**
author, *Miraculous Living*

"This wonderful book will help you live a meaningful life. Don't let the title fool you. This book is filled with the wisdom of the ages."

—**Bernie S. Siegel, M.D.**
author, *Love, Medicine & Miracles*

"A thoughtful and inspiring book for any traveler on the spiritual path."

—**Barbara De Angelis, Ph.D.**
author, *Are You the One for Me?*

"The easy informality of this deeply sensitive, insightful work by one of today's outstanding Jewish spiritual guides dispels the obfuscation that too often surrounds authentic Jewish mysticism. Those who have been thrilled and inspired by New Age ideas will find here a wealth of sound, practical guidance as to how to pursue their visions through forms and concepts that are truly rooted in the ancient Jewish tradition yet sparklingly relevant to the needs and challenges of our time."

—**Rabbi Avraham Greenbaum**
author, *The Wings of the Sun*

"This is the book I've been waiting for! *New Age Judaism* is a beautiful, heartfelt and wonderfully embracing invitation to step to the highest rung of spirituality. I recommend this heartily to anyone seeking to pierce to the core of Jewish wisdom and universal truth."

—Alan Cohen
author, *A Deep Breath of Life*

"Bridging the old and the new—linking past, present and future—is the call of our time. In *New Age Judaism*, Melinda Ribner does a remarkable job of interfacing ageless Jewish spirituality with the New-Age life today. She creates what perhaps can be coined "The New New Age." For that, we owe her and her book a deep debt of gratitude."

—Rabbi Simon Jacobson
author, *Toward a Meaningful Life*,
director of The Meaningful Life Center

"Mindy Ribner is one of the main heirs of the spiritual legacy of the legendary Rabbi Shlomo Carlebach, who gave her *smicha* (authorization) as a meditation teacher. In *New Age Judaism*, Mindy teaches us the deepest depths of mysticism and meditation, of Kabbalah and self-knowledge. Her words contain an echo *(bat kol)* of the *Shechinah;* her kabbalistic meditations are both practical and powerful. Mindy, a premier teacher of authentic Jewish meditation, is one of the great lights of this generation."

—Yitzhak Buxbaum
author, *Jewish Spiritual Practices*

"Rebbe Herschel Ziditchover, the great kabbalist and miracle worker who lived two hundred years ago, was asked what the Baal Shem Tov revealed that was not already revealed by Rabbi Shimeon Bar Yochai and Rabbi Yitzchok Luria, also known as the Arizel. The rebbe explained that the *Zohar,* written by Rabbi Shimeon Bar Yochai, showed the world that there is a God who rules Creation. The Arizel taught us how to connect to God, and the Baal Shem Tov showed us that God is everywhere. Now, in the spirit of these great luminaries, Mindy comes to ignite the light of our own souls so the darkness of our time is lifted, and we can truly see God everywhere and experience Judaism as a path of great joy. *New Age Judaism* is illuminating."

—Rabbi Yidel Stein
Brisker Synagogue, Williamsburg, New York

NEW AGE JUDAISM

ANCIENT WISDOM FOR THE MODERN WORLD

Melinda Ribner

SIMCHA PRESS
An Imprint of Health Communications, Inc.

Deerfield Beach, Florida
www.simchapress.com

Library of Congress Cataloging-in-Publication Data

Ribner, Melinda.
    New Age Judaism : ancient wisdom for the modern world /
Melinda Ribner.
        p.   cm.
    ISBN 1-55874-789-3
    1. Spiritual life—Judaism. 2. Self-actualization (Psychology)—
Religious aspects—Judaism. 3. Cabala. 4. Meditation—Judaism.
5. New Age movement. I. Title.
BM723.R53 1999
296.7—dc21

                                                                98-053969

Publisher: Simcha Press
            An Imprint of Health Communications, Inc.
            3201 S.W. 15th Street
            Deerfield Beach, Florida 33442-8190

Cover design by Andrea Perrine Brower
Inside book design by Dawn Grove

New Age Judaism is dedicated

to all those who dream of a New Age,

a world filled with love

for all people and love for the Holy One.

אני מסכימה ללמד

עולם רואה קולות

Behold! Days are coming, says God, when I will make a "new covenant" with the House of Israel and the House of Judah. Not like the covenant that I made with their ancestors, when I redeemed them from Egypt. . . . This is the covenant. . . . I will place My Torah within them and inscribe it upon their hearts (Jer. 31:30-32).

CONTENTS

PART ONE: MEDITATIVE KABBALAH

PART TWO: JEWISH SELF-HELP

PART THREE: THE NEW AGE IS _SO_ JEWISH

ACKNOWLEDGMENTS
AND BLESSINGS

I want to thank Steve Shraggis of Carol Publishing, my first publisher, who asked me to write a book with this title and left the content totally up to me. I thank Kim Weiss, my new publisher, for selecting this book to be one of the first books to initiate the new venture of Simcha Press. May Simcha Press be blessed to bring much joy to the world. I also thank Carolyn Jarashaw for making the connection for me with Kim.

When beginning to acknowledge the people who have supported me Jewishly, I first have to acknowledge and thank my teachers of blessed memory, my father Isaac Ribner, Yitzchok Ben Avraham, my Rabbis Shlomo Carlebach and Yitzchok Kirzner, who nourished and sustained me in the early years. Without their support, I do not know if I would have been able to stand as the Jew. May their souls be lifted up in the merit of this book.

I want to acknowledge and thank my rabbis, Rabbi Mordecai Tendler and Rabbi Simon Jacobson; my healer, Michael Assedo; and my dear rabbi friends, Rabbis Yidel Stein, Zwe Padeh, Avraham Newman, Dovid Sears, Yitzchok Ring and Maggid Yitzchok Buzbaum, who have learned with me over the years, who have been there for me on a personal level, and who, mostly, have inspired me by their love and devotion to

Torah. Each of you in your own life brings so much goodness to the world. May each of you continue to shine.

I also thank my immediate family, my mother, my brother, Stephen, and my Uncle Richard Ribner, or Uncle Sunny as we call him, for the love, support and encouragement given to me over the years. I have been truly blessed to be linked to each of you in such an intimate way. May God continue to bless all of us with good health, more joy, and additions to our loving family.

And mostly I thank my circle of loving and devoted students, who have been with me for many years. Together we have paved new pathways into Torah and have grown in the ways we want most for ourselves. With your encouragement and support, I have continued to teach. We have been truly blessed by our association. May we expand our circle so as to share our blessings with more people. May we continue to grow in love and awe of God.

And ultimately, in the deepest places in my heart and soul, I must acknowledge that I feel a deep gratitude and awe before God who has blessed me with the privilege of imparting Jewish meditation and meditative kabbalah, and with the opportunity to share myself with so many more people through the medium of this book.

AUTHOR TO READER

Many people will be surprised to find that Judaism is fundamentally aligned with what we think of today as the New Age. Many of the beliefs and practices we associate with the New Age are not new but are part of kabbalah, the Jewish mystical tradition. Kabbalah, a Hebrew word that literally means "to receive," is a repository of esoteric knowledge and spiritual practices received through prophecy, elucidated and protected by the leaders of the Jewish lineage for thousands of years. Though this knowledge has been mostly closeted throughout time, kabbalah is becoming increasingly popular and available today. Kabbalah has important and relevant information to reveal about meditation, angels, vegetarianism, holistic healing, personal transformation, unity consciousness and much else that concerns the New Age movement.

New Age Judaism is not about another modified form of Judaism to meet the needs of the moment. The teachings presented here are authentic, eternal and universal. *New Age Judaism* actually makes age-old Judaism's traditional and kabbalistic teachings accessible in a new way. These teachings address the deepest questions that have always troubled humans from ancient times to the present, and they provide guidance in how to live happier and more fulfilling lives. Most people today have been deprived of this wisdom. Many of us have looked for spiritual truth and mystical experience in India, Japan and elsewhere, never even knowing that a treasure chest of riches was available in our own spiritual backyards.

New Age Judaism is not so much a scholarly work as it is a very practical guidebook to Jewish spirituality that includes many insights and personal observations from my own spiritual journey in Judaism. As a person steeped in traditional Judaism as well as New Age culture for twenty years, I have a unique, intimate and broad understanding of both worlds. *New Age Judaism* provides a synthesis of Jewish and New Age thought and spiritual practice to enable the reader to receive the best of both. This book is for anyone who seeks to probe the secrets of life. From the religiously devout and spiritually minded to the New Age or secular Jew and non-Jew, each person will find spiritual nourishment. Though grounded in the Jewish mystical and prophetic tradition, these teachings are radical. They may challenge some of your concepts of God, yourself and life, and encourage you to grow in ways you most want for yourself.

Deep within, beneath the veils of modern sophistication we wear, many of us may still envision God as we were taught as children. We were taught to conceive of God as some kind of human figure, usually an old man with a long white beard, who sits on a throne and autocratically dispenses judgments, rewarding and punishing our every move. The Bible itself at times speaks of God as a human being. He gets angry and jealous, and He punishes us. Who would want to come close to this God? Yet we are told to both love and fear this God.

Our parents may have used these images to control us as vulnerable children. If we are good, everything will be good. If we suffer, it may mean that we did something wrong and God is punishing us. If I was criticized as a child by my parents and grew up feeling that I was not good enough, I may project these feelings onto God. I may feel unlovable. Not feeling worthy of having a relationship with God, I may be fearful or rejecting of God. If I grew up with ambivalent and inconsistent caring on the part of my parents, I may experience God as equally absent or unreliable. Many people carry around a lot of anger about the suffering they experienced in their lives, and they blame God. Their anger makes it hard to open up to God. Unless we have studied kabbalah and meditated intensively, and really worked on ourselves, our images of God will be contaminated by our childhood experience of our parents. Our parents were God's representatives to us.

As we mature, we begin to realize that life is not so simple. Life is not black and white. God is not a sugar daddy or a dictatorial tyrant. If we are to grow in spiritual awareness and responsibility as adults, it is necessary that we let go of some of the childish beliefs and projections we have about God and the limiting ideas we have about who we are. We are no longer helpless or powerless children. Why should we limit or allow ourselves to be limited in this way?

Because of past negative associations with the word "God," many of my students prefer to refer to God with the kabbalistic Hebrew term for God, *Ain Sof,* which means "without limit," or with a phrase such as "Higher Reality," "Inner Reality" or "Cosmic Consciousness." Judaism has many names for God, referring to God's various attributes. In everyday conversation, religious Jews routinely call God *Hashem,* which means "the Name."

Rabbi Simon Jacobson, author of *Towards a Meaningful Life,* shared an interesting anecdote relating to the difficulty many people experience with the word "God." When he began teaching, he used terms such as "Higher Reality," "True Reality," "Cosmic Intelligence" and "Inner Essence" in place of the word "God." After some time, one of his students asked him privately if he was talking about God when he used those terms. Rabbi Jacobson confided that he was, but he said,

"Don't tell the others. It will spoil class for them."

It might be helpful for those of you who carry a lot of baggage regarding the word "God" to use terms such as "Ultimate Reality" or "True Reality" or "Cosmic Intelligence" instead. Even if you do not have trouble with the word "God," you might want to experiment with this. You will find doing so transformational. Consider whether the following questions elicit a different response within you: "Do you want to come close to or know God?" or "Do you want to come close to or know the Inner Reality?"

There is a big debate among Jews as to whether God should be referred to as male or female. I want to address this concern at the outset of the book and even beg you not to let this pose a barrier for you. I know that many of you reading this book may be uncomfortable with my referring to God as male, as I do. Jewish traditional and kabbalistic teachings inform us that God is neither male nor female, though God has masculine and feminine characteristics. I personally prefer to refer to God in the masculine. Many people feel differently, and that is perfectly acceptable. Highlighting the masculinity of God enables me to connect to the traditional practice of the majority of Jews and to relate more easily to God as a lover. It awakens more devotion and willingness to serve within me. Traditionally, God is viewed as the bridegroom and Israel as the bride. Before God, we all have to be women.

Some people have been turned off to Judaism by the apparent domination of men in religious synagogue life. Gender issues have played a significant factor in dividing the Jewish people into various denominations. Feelings are so strong that Jews affiliated with one group are not comfortable praying in a congregation of another. There has been increasing tension within the Jewish community as a result. I believe that this is most unfortunate, and painful. Whether women are counted in the *minyan* (quorum for prayer), whether they participate equally in the service, whether they sit together with men or

they sit apart has great significance for many people. I suspect
that it is not so important to God. We hear repeatedly from the
prophets that God is less concerned with the external performance of rituals than with inner motivation. God wants your
heart.

It is tragic that religion, which has the unique power to unite
people in love and community, has too often divided people
into camps of believers and nonbelievers. Religious wars, persecution and seething but unfounded hatred between groups
have been supported in the name of God. Wars are still being
fought today in the name of Allah. We must bear in mind that
hatred and prejudice in the name of religion is not God's way.
Such thinking represents an old spiritual paradigm that has
separated people from each other, and from God. If God is perceived as remote, somewhere in heaven and separate from
people, then people experience themselves as separate from
each other. Many openhearted, loving people have been alienated from following a religious spiritual path because they
could not bear the divisiveness of religion. It is painful and
offensive to sensitive, compassionate people to listen to
sermons of narrow-mindedness, prejudice and arrogance
dished out in the name of God.

Most traditional religions reinforce the belief that God is in-
accessible, judgmental and prejudiced. Unfortunately, every religion claims that it has the exclusive truth about God and its way
is the most beautiful, most efficacious path to God—and if not the
only, certainly the best. Each religion informs a person what he or
she should do, say and think in order to have a good life and a
good place in the afterlife. Implicit is the threat of negative
consequences for failure to comply with religious dictates.

I do not want to be critical of religion. I love religion. I
have been religiously observant for twenty years. I want to
testify from my own personal experience that today, in this
world, imperfect as it is, a person can experience great joy and

spiritual ecstasy on the Jewish path. I believe religion is a vital component of every person's life. I believe that every religion offers powerful spiritual riches, tremendous depths and mysteries but that, sadly, the deep spirituality at the heart of religion is rarely transmitted. This transmission must be received from a person who embodies these teachings, not from an institution. Kabbalah was always transmitted directly from a teacher to a student. The Chassidic movement within Judaism taught that every Jew must have a rebbe, a spiritual teacher dedicated to cultivating the potential of his students and initiating them into Jewish spiritual practice.

Unfortunately, when religions became institutionalized, their teachers and representatives were trained to transmit dogma and beliefs, but generally they were not initiated into the mystical practices at the heart of their religions. This is true for Judaism as well. Rabbis spend a lot of time learning things that they will never be able to share with their congregations. Their own spiritual experiences may be very limited. They may be Torah scholars and masters of ancient holy texts, but—regrettably—rabbis are not trained to be spiritual teachers, counselors and healers. This is unfortunate, for teachers cannot share what they have not received. Furthermore, if teachers are not personally familiar with the terrain of mystical and transpersonal experiences, they will not be able to provide good counsel to those who have been blessed in this way.

When I studied in a religious yeshiva twenty years ago, I was told not to think too much, to follow the prescriptions of Jewish law and not expect spiritual joy or mystical experience because people are on such a low level today, but if I were observant, I would be rewarded with spiritual ecstasy in the next world. These teachers, religiously observant from childhood, apparently had little spiritual experience themselves. They may have been threatened by my intense spiritual yearning and desire for mystical experience.

It is no coincidence that the New Age movement, which emphasizes unity and tolerance, springs forth in the United States, a place where individual freedom and democracy are valued. New Age is a popular term—almost cliché in our time—yet it is difficult to define exactly what the teachings of the New Age movement are. Sprouting forth during the counter-culture of the 1960s, the New Age movement is an evolving grass-roots movement. Some readers will remember the popular 1960s musical *Hair,* which proclaimed that humanity is entering the Age of Aquarius where peace and harmony will reign forever. This is the heralding of the New Age, which can be witnessed in the writings of Marilyn Ferguson, Fritjof Capra, Jean Houston and Rabbi Zalman Schachter-Shalomi, who have all written about the emerging spiritual paradigm of unity con-sciousness. Surely everyone can acknowledge that we are in the midst of major changes that permeate every level of our being.

The traditional spiritual paradigm—which emphasized humans as separate from the world, as well as separate from God—shaped our approaches to science and medicine, not just religion. For hundreds of years our world view was gov-erned by the dualistic philosophy of Descartes and the physics of Isaac Newton, which viewed the world as a great cosmic machine that could be manipulated. Employing this mecha-nistic perspective resulted in many dramatic technological advances in our external material world; however, the price was the devaluing of humanity's inner world. In the process of conquering the material world, we objectified and compart-mentalized ourselves and our relationships. The quality of our inner life deteriorated. Today we have much material comfort, yet we are starving spiritually and are more vulnerable to anxi-ety, depression and mental illness than ever before. We are more isolated these days. We have networks, not communities. Relationships between people, between husband and wife, children and parents, friends and coworkers, have suffered. There is more divorce. Our environment has been damaged. People are calling out for a new way of being, and our prayers are being answered.

Kabbalah predicted that the New Age would be accompanied by tremendous breakthroughs in science and technology. Einstein's discoveries and recent breakthroughs in quantum physics have begun a paradigm shift that has taken us away from the concept of a lifeless mechanistic universe that we can manipulate to our own needs to an alive, intelligent, responsive interactive universe of which we are an integral part. I remember reading a long time ago that Einstein discovered his theories, such as $E = mc^2$, in a dream state. To me, his revelations appear to have been a kind of prophetic experience. The way the language of the new physics describes the world is strikingly similar to that of kabbalah. As you read this book, you will see that the concepts of God, human and world revealed and understood in kabbalah are closely aligned with that of the New Age perspective and that of the emerging science. Modern physics is looking for a unified field theory that will explain all phenomena. Physicists sense that there is a unifying energy beyond the level of subatomic particles that holds everything together. It appears that modern physicists are looking for God, though they might not state it that way. In kabbalah, God is the underlying factor that unifies everything in Creation. Today, science and spirituality, once opposed to each other, are beginning to speak the same language.

As we begin to recognize the bankruptcy of the old paradigm, we are being given a new emerging paradigm that is monistic, holistic and more gentle than how we lived before. It offers a new way to experience ourselves and life. *New Age Judaism* contains many powerful teachings and meditation practices to help usher in this new consciousness. Like its author and reflective of the transition period in which this book is written,

New Age Judaism blends New Age, kabbalistic and traditional material. As a people, and as individuals, we are still in the process of leaving the old and have not totally arrived at the new. We are at the crossroads. I believe and experience that we are being given tremendous heavenly support to enter into a New Age, a time when love and unity will replace the fear and separatism inherent in the old spiritual paradigm.

As we move further into the New Age, we will find our focus shifting to the integration of physicality and spirituality. Public conversation will be less about accumulating more material possessions or even how to cope with stress and more about how to be an integrated, whole and spiritual person. Having achieved so much materially, we also have experienced the bankruptcy of materialism and learned that having more does not make a person happier. We have witnessed that our heroes—the movie stars, politicians and wealthy who seemed to have mastered the material world—no longer model the good life appropriately for us. After so much emphasis placed on materialism, in the New Age we will find that who we are will be more important than how much money we earn or how famous we are.

We are discovering, often the hard way, that our happiness must be found inside. We are experiencing an emerging social climate of greater openness and greater public interest in spirituality. Today, people can be less fearful of ridicule and more open with others about personal spiritual experiences. It is no longer considered weird to be spiritually or mystically oriented. Even today's movie stars seek the counsel of spiritual teachers. Personal spiritual experience is becoming increasingly more desirable and valuable than material possessions.

Meditation is the doorway to the unity consciousness of the New Age. I sincerely question whether a person will be able to let go of the old limiting spiritual paradigm without a dedicated practice of meditation. Meditation is popular in the New Age because meditation provides the experience for a holistic inner knowing that is much greater than what we can experience through intellect alone. Meditation synthesizes the right and left hemispheres of the brain. (The right hemisphere of the brain is the intuitive part of the human mind, and the left brain hemisphere is the cognitive part.) When both come together, this is a true knowing experience. In Hebrew, "to know" is "to become one with." We become one with what we meditate upon. *New Age Judaism* presents and discusses the deepest kabbalistic teachings about God and life and the powerful meditative and kabbalistic practices that can be used to achieve a high state of God and unity consciousness.

It is very auspicious that the ancient forms of meditation and spiritual teachings within all ancient religious traditions, which were hidden for thousands of years, are being revived and widely disseminated at this time. It is not just proponents of the New Age who feel hopeful that we are at the dawn of a new age, the Aquarian Age, where peace and unity will prevail. Prominent Jewish leaders also believe that we are living in auspicious times and that the ancient prophecies of the long-awaited New Age will be fulfilled in our time. Christian fundamentalists are also anticipating an imminent second coming of Jesus, which they believe will usher in a New Age. *New Age Judaism* offers some of the ancient prophecies describing this New Age from a Jewish perspective so you can be more prepared for the predicted changes ahead of us. Jews have been talking about and preparing for this time for thousands of years.

I am primarily a teacher of Jewish meditation. This is my spiritual calling. My real talent lies not in writing but in facilitating and imparting meditation. I have taught Jewish meditation for more than sixteen years. I have taught at synagogues, religious academic associations of all affiliations and New Age health centers. Through my own organization, The

Jewish Meditation Circle, I have worked with a continuing group of students for over ten years, and that has afforded me a wonderful opportunity to explore kabbalistic meditation in greater depth. My classes have been attended by Jews of all affiliations, as well as non-Jews. I am happy that my work has had a wide range of appeal.

In my beginning classes in Jewish meditation, I use meditation as a vehicle for imparting spiritual teachings so that people can experience and integrate them more easily into their lives. I believe that meditation is one of the most powerful tools for personal transformation and increased spiritual awareness. It is the greatest gift that you can give yourself. It reduces stress and helps you feel better about yourself, and it also opens you to a depth of spirituality that you cannot enter otherwise. For this reason, meditation exercises are interspersed throughout this book.

Many of the great Jewish sages and teachers claimed to have reached spiritual heights through meditation. Although the practice of Jewish meditation is ancient, there were special times throughout history when its practice was more widespread, and this brought much blessing upon the Jewish people and the world. The most meaningful time occurred during the days of worship at the ancient temple in Jerusalem when, the Talmud says, over a million people meditated. It is said the Jewish people enjoyed a closer relationship with God then. I believe that the special relationship and availability of the Divine Presence then and now may be attributed to the widespread practice of meditation. I believe and I hope that as more and more Jews meditate, the Divine Presence will once again become more tangible, ushering in the New Age that Judaism has prophesied.

Though this book draws on a range of Mussar, Chassidic, and kabbalistic sources such as Bachya Ibn Paquda, Maimonides, Moses Nachmanides, Rabbi Moses Chaim Luzzatto, Rabbi

Nachman of Breslov, and Rabbi Schneur Zalman of Lubavitch, it is my great honor and privilege to highlight the teachings of two of the greatest Jewish saints: Rabbi Yitzchok Luria and the Baal Shem Tov. Both ushered in periods of Jewish renewal and revival that continue to resonate today. Both meditated extensively and taught meditation to their followers. As we live in a time of Jewish renewal, their teachings and practices are particularly relevant.

Rabbi Yitzchok Luria, more commonly known as the Arizel, an acronym for Elohi Rabbi Isaac, lived from 1534 to 1572. Though many Jewish teachers were considered and even called holy, he was the only one who was called godly. His closest disciples saw him as an angel. By the time Yitzchok Luria was eight years old, he was recognized as a child prodigy who had mastered Talmud. It is said he discovered the *Zohar,* a principal text of Jewish mysticism, at the age of seventeen and that it became a vehicle for meditation for him. He devoted fifteen years to meditation, first with his teacher Rabbi Betzalel and then by himself. He spent the last two of those years meditating alone in a hut on the Nile. According to legend, he was taught by Elijah, the Prophet, who commanded him to go to Israel to teach others. He journeyed and lived in Safed, Israel, for a brief period of time and taught only a few people, mostly those who were already knowledgeable in kabbalah. Though his principal student, Rabbi Hayim Vital, studied with him for only eighteen months, Rabbi Vital faithfully recorded the teachings of Rabbi Luria in volumes of books. My friend Rabbi Zwe Padeh has recently published the first English translation of these teachings of Rabbi Yitzchok Luria as recorded in the kabbalistic masterpiece called *Etz Hayim: Tree of Life.* The kabbalistic teachings of the Arizel have been widely accepted by Jewish kabbalists, and some of his teachings and practices have infiltrated mainstream Jewish life.

The Baal Shem Tov, whose name translates as "Master of the

Good Name," is more well-known than Rabbi Yitzchok Luria. The Baal Shem Tov, who lived from 1698 to 1760, was the founder of the Chassidic movement, which revitalized Judaism in eastern Europe. The Baal Shem Tov was orphaned early, probably when he was around six years of age, and spent years meditating in seclusion before he began teaching at the age of thirty-six. The Baal Shem Tov lived at a time when Jewish life was not much different than it is now. Some very knowledge-able people were steeped in traditional Jewish learning while thousands of Jews were spiritually deprived. There was little spiritual sustenance for the latter.

The Baal Shem Tov delivered a very simple message that is as important and potentially revolutionary now as it was then. He actually did not teach anything new; rather, he made acces-sible the underlying and basic teachings of Judaism that people had forgotten or failed to emphasize. The Baal Shem Tov proclaimed the unity of God and taught what this really meant. Though recognizing the transcendence of God, the Baal Shem Tov emphasized the immanence of God, making people aware that Godliness pervades all aspects of life and is accessible to every openhearted person, Jew and non-Jew. God and holiness are not just a part of Torah learning and religious observance, but God is in life. Through an open heart, an aver-age person can sometimes experience Godliness in a purer, more profound way than a learned person who is stuck in his head.

The Baal Shem Tov also emphasized the belief in Divine Providence; that is, God is interacting with every detail of people's lives. God is renewing everything and everyone con-stantly. He also emphasized joy in service: "Serve God with gladness," as Psalm 100 says. Seeing Godliness in everything naturally fills a person with joy. The Baal Shem Tov taught people how to be joyous, and he was an extraordinary miracle maker who helped people on many levels. He also possessed many extraordinary healing powers, not only of physical diseases, but even of past-life karma.

The Baal Shem Tov recorded in a letter to his brother-in-law an extraordinary mystical experience of soul ascension wherein he was transported to a wondrous spiritual world. There he saw many souls, some living and some dead, who were experiencing various levels of Godliness. He was encouraged to go even higher until he entered the chamber of the Messiah. He was not sure then whether he was living or had passed away. He was told that he had not died, but that he gave great pleasure on high by bringing about unification through the Holy Torah. The Baal Shem Tov spoke directly to the Messiah and asked him when he would come. The Messiah replied, "It will be at a time when your teachings become widespread in the world." The Baal Shem Tov reported that he was surprised and distressed to hear this because he knew that it would take a long time for such a thing to happen. During the Baal Shem Tov's soul-ascent experience, the Messiah taught him many things that he could not reveal, but the Baal Shem Tov did relay that the Messiah encouraged us to make unifications in all aspects of our lives. It is the intention of this book to make the teachings of the Baal Shem Tov accessible to many more people so as to quicken the time of the New Age.

With all its laws and rituals, Judaism is essentially about unifying the soul and the body, God and the world. There is great joy in this, for it brings wholeness to a person and a feeling of oneness with other people. It is my prayer that you, my dear reader, experience greater harmony in your relationships, inner peace, health and spiritual vibrancy as a result of reading this book and by practicing the meditations it contains. May *New Age Judaism* bring unification and enrichment to your life.

PART ONE

MEDITATIVE KABBALAH

1

WHO, WHAT AND WHERE IS GOD?

Many people wonder and question "Where is God?" There is a natural yearning within each of us for God, for a taste of eternity. We search in many places and in many ways for the transcendent experience. Yet the deepest truth is that everything we are looking for is available within us. God is within us. We have each been given a pure and holy soul. This soul is our true essence and is actually a part of God.

It is elevating but not necessary that we travel to holy places to find God. We can stand at one of the holiest sites in the world and feel absolutely nothing. It is possible to not feel anything wherever we are if our hearts are closed. We can be in our own home and feel the Divine Presence in a powerfully intense way. The Baal Shem Tov said that people are where their thoughts are. If we are in Jerusalem with a mind not filled with holiness, we are not really in Jerusalem. Our body may be there, but we are not. Similarly, if we are in New York and we're pining for God, we really are in God's holy city.

I recently returned from conducting a weeklong retreat at a Jewish Renewal center, during which a young woman gave a moving testimony about her experience. Before she took the workshop, she explained, when asked where she *davened,* where she prayed, she would be embarrassed to tell people "nowhere." She was ashamed that she did not have a personal connection to God and was uncomfortable attending any synagogue. During the workshop she opened to a very deep and personal connection to God. She proudly announced that henceforth when asked where she davens she will respond "everywhere." At every moment, in every place, in every activity, there is an opportunity to connect directly with God.

God is wherever we open to Him, so close to us we cannot see Him. Sometimes we wish that God were physical, so we could feel and touch Him, but then God would be separate from us. If God were physical, He would be limited to time and space, would occupy one space and therefore not be in another space. There can never be a total merger between things that are physical, because each one occupies its own space. God can be so close to us because God is not physical. God is everywhere, but to experience God, we need to let God into our lives. Meditation, prayer and doing good deeds to connect with God's Will create the channels to spiritually open, purify and expand our consciousness. If we are full of ourselves, we will not be open to the experience of God. We need to empty ourselves and allow God to be in us and with us. If we are open, we will feel God's presence within us for we are a part of God. We live in the midst of God.

Because God is not physical and does not occupy space and time in the way that we do, it is not surprising that many may question God's existence. Even fervent God-believers are sometimes troubled with doubts and lapses in faith. *Duties of the Heart,* the wonderful classic book of Jewish philosophy by Bachya Ibn Paquda, which I highly recommend, provides the following illustration to prove the existence of God: Can you imagine pouring ink onto a blank sheet of paper and forming the most beautiful poetry? Everyone has to acknowledge that this is impossible. Similarly, how can this world not have a Creator?

All too often we are so busy that we fail to appreciate all the goodness we are given merely in being alive. It is good to set aside a few moments periodically from time to time, especially when you are outside, to close your eyes, take some slow deep breaths and allow the mind to quiet. With each inhalation, feel yourself open to greater vitality. With each exhalation, allow yourself to relax. Pause between each breath. When you have stilled the mental chatter sufficiently to be present to yourself as you inhale and exhale, open your eyes and look around you. See this world as if for the first time. What a beautiful world! How could this universe, which is so magnificent, so intricately designed and so complex, not have a Creator who loves His Creation?

We do not always see God in the way we see physical things in this world, but that does not mean that God does not exist. The *Zohar* calls God "The Most Hidden of All the Hidden." God is concealed and hidden in our physical world. Many things exist that we cannot see or touch, and we rely increasingly on them in our daily life. For example, I have not seen electricity or radio waves, yet I assume that they exist because I see how I benefit from them. Very few of us have any real understanding of how television, the telephone or the Internet operates, yet we have come to depend on them. Acknowledging our acceptance of the unknown working in our lives helps us more easily accept the presence of an invisible, all-pervasive God.

Though most people believe in the existence of a Creator, some feel that God is distant from us. It is true that God is hidden, but God is not distant. God is simply awaiting your heartfelt invitation to enter your life. God is very humble and does not want to impose the Divine Presence upon anyone unless they really want it. The Kotzer Rebbe reminds us, "God is where you let Him in." God's love and accessibility are emphasized in Jewish thought and practice, and the legacy of the Jewish prophets reminds us of just that. The prophet Isaiah tells us, "All the world is full of His glory." The prophet Jeremiah quotes God as saying, "Do I not fill heaven and earth?"

The fundamental belief in the existence and unity of God is the most essential point in Judaism. Everything is predicated upon it. Judaism is most acknowledged for bringing to the world the concept of monotheism, the belief in one God. The Hebrew word for Israel, which is *Yisrael,* may be broken into two root words: *Yeshar* and *El,* which together mean "straight to God." The Jew goes straight to God. Through time Judaism developed its own bureaucratic structures, but in its essence Judaism remains antiauthoritarian. The Jew prays

directly to the Creator of the Universe. There is no need for intermediaries, rabbis or idols before the one God. Each Jew is potentially a high priest, bringing down blessings for self and others.
People identifying with the New Age should be comfortable with this
basic tenet of Judaism: Every person, regardless of stature or religion, can have a personal relationship with God. Each of us can talk
directly to God and our words make a difference. According to
Judaism, even non-Jews can be prophets and can be filled with the
holy spirit. The Divine Presence is not discriminatory.

According to most important and basic Jewish teachings, the one
and only God created this world and He did so to bestow goodness.
When God finished creating everything in this world, the Bible says,
"God saw that it was good." After God created man, the Bible says,
"God saw all that He had made, and behold it was very good." We
human beings were made in a manner unlike all previous creations.
We were made in the likeness and image of God. We were made to
be capable of receiving the highest goodness, which is God. A partial
good would not be sufficient for humans. In his book *The Way of
God,* one of the explanations given by Moses Luzzatto for God proclaiming the creation of man as "very good" is that man was given
free will. Of all the creatures God created in this world, we human
beings alone can choose to come close to God. God wants us to
choose Him, yet it has to be our choice. God blesses us in many
ways in life, but God's greatest blessing is that God allows us to be
attached to Him and, in that way, experience our own perfection.

Let's understand this exalted state of consciousness with a simple
example from our human experience. Imagine that a person gives
you a gift. The gift is wonderful and beautiful in its own right. It is a
great pleasure to receive such a gift. If you love the person who gave
you the gift, you are happier to receive it than if you received it from
someone you didn't have strong feelings for. Because the giver loves
and knows you, the gift is exactly what you need at this time. The
gift's real value, however, is that it is an expression of this person's
love. It is the love of this person that is really important to you. This
is what you really want. If this person gives you the opportunity
to come close, to love and to know him intimately, this is the greatest gift. Similarly, God gives us many gifts in our lives, but God's

greatest gift and blessing is that we can know and love Him. It was for this we were created. God wanted to be known and to be loved.

Devekut, "cleaving to God," is the goal of all Jewish spiritual practice. The righteous and holy people of the Jewish lineage cling to God and identify with Him in such a way that they experience themselves as part of God and are able to share in the ecstasy and pleasure that God experiences within Himself. Such people shine Godliness in this world, inspire and model the spiritual potential that is within each of us. Through actively attaching ourselves to God, we expand our consciousness and are able to receive the highest good and the greatest joy. When we make a God-connection, we have more love in our hearts for all of Creation, including ourselves. To access our own tremendous spiritual potential, Judaism directs us to seek God at all times, to love God, to serve God, and to walk in His ways, even though we cannot know with our minds who and what God is.

In his desire for increasing intimacy and knowledge of God, Moses, the most exalted Jewish prophet, asked God directly, "What is your name? Who are You?" God answered, *"Ehyeh, Asher Ehyeh,"* which means, "I will be what I will be." What a name! It is considered, kabbalistically, to be the name closest to the essence of God. Will is the highest expression of the Divine. God created the world because it was His will and desire to do so and for no other reason. It was not that God was deficient and needed the world to complete Him. The name "I will be what I will be" tells us that God is totally free and does not depend on anything else. No deficiency can be attributed to His existence. This is the only time in the Torah that this name is revealed. God is telling us that He is not definable. "I will be what I will be." God is not a fixed or finished product, like an idol, but is very much alive, living and evolving. As Rabbi Zalman Schachter-Shalomi and David Cooper said, "God is a verb. God is being God."

Interestingly enough, the most familiar name of God, YHVH, is rooted in the Hebrew word *hovey,* which means "to be." When the Hebrew letter *yud* is placed in front of the root, it makes the verb active. So YHVH means "active being." YHVH is Being being. It is existence itself. God was, is and will be. In Hebrew, God is the only being that can say "I am." For example, a person who is hungry would say in Hebrew "I hungry." God is ultimately the only true reality. God is what makes everything else alive. The Torah, to inform us that our lives are tied to this God-connection, tells us, "He who attaches himself to YHVH is alive today." God is life. We are more vibrant and alive when we make a God-connection. To the extent we open to God, we open to life, to reality and to our true selves. God is the "stuff" of existence itself, and we are part of God. Much like electricity that empowers our machines, God is the fuel of existence for everything.

It is important to know that everything that is known about God is about how we experience God and how God relates to us. It is said that God is good or God is loving, but this describes God in relation to us. This is not about God as God is to Himself. This is beyond us. I reiterate this point because it is essential. Once this is understood, many crises of faith may be avoided. People struggle with their own limited concepts of God, not with God. The true God-believer has much in common with the agnostic, for both acknowledge that they can never know God. We must always bear in mind that our own concepts of God are limited, therefore we have no right to impose them upon others who may have different concepts than we do. We are all a creation of God. We are finite, bound by time and space. Can a part know the whole? Our experience of God is limited. Can we who are limited and finite know that which is infinite? God is even more than what is infinite. God is beyond all conceptualization and definition. God created concepts. Even if we describe God as infinite, infinity is still a concept. It is not God. As my teacher Reb Shlomo Carlebach would often say with a sigh, "What do we know?"

We all have a tendency to create images of God to help us relate to Him. We often think of God as a person. God is the father, the mother, the friend, the lover. This is natural and helpful, but if we are stuck in our images, we will never experience God as God. We only experience our own projections. This is a very important point to remember. God in His essence is beyond every definition, concept or image we may have about Him. We may have a preference to refer to God as male or as female, to call God "King" or "Queen," or to eliminate all reference to gender and call God "Source of Life,"

"Universal Consciousness" or "Limitless Light," but these are merely our preferences.

Unfortunately, we too often let our images of God separate us from the experience of God—and from each other. We benefit when we remember that our images are only images, not God. The third commandment actually forbids the making of images or pictures of God because God cannot be visualized or imagined. The Bible says, "Man is created in the image and likeness of God." The only image we may have of God is the human being.

Even though we can never achieve complete knowledge of God, we are encouraged to consciously apply ourselves to learning about God. Learning Torah and its commentaries and studying the prayers written by the great Jewish prophets and the teachings of Jewish saints will teach us much about God and awaken love for Him. As the song goes, "To know him is to love him." Studying and following the path prescribed by Jewish law teaches us how to bring God-awareness into our daily lives. The most direct and powerful opportunity we have to learn about God comes from our own prayer, meditation and life experiences, but even from such secular studies as science and psychology we also learn about God.

We are privileged to live at a time of tremendous breakthroughs of knowledge in all areas of life. As we as individuals and as a society progress in learning, in understanding ourselves as well as the laws of the universe, we learn more about God and the possibilities of life are expanded. Yet there will always be more to uncover. We will never be able to say that we know God or His world completely.

Similarly, because our souls are a part of God, it is also important to know that we can never even say that we know ourselves or another person completely. When we get to know other people as they are, and not as we want them to be, we will see that they are more than we originally imagined. We should suspend all limiting ideas about ourselves and people, for there are awesome depths of beauty and majesty within every person for every person is in essence a Divine Soul in a human body. Some of us may need more polishing so our souls shine more brightly. Some of us may need better eyes so we can see the holy sweet souls within others. Nevertheless, as we open to experience the depths of our own souls, we bear witness that all humans, including ourselves, were created in the image and likeness of God. In those moments, we taste Godliness in ourselves and others. This is true intimacy.

To truly come close to God, to experience God's oneness, to gain a glimpse of who we are, to be fully alive, we have to let go of our limiting concepts of God and self and go deep inside, to the innermost places of our being. Meditate and meditate. God says, "Be still, and know that I am God"(Psalm 46). When we quiet our minds and open our hearts, God's voice may be heard, God's love may be experienced. This is the gift of meditation. *Sefer Yetzirah: The Book of Formation,* which is thousands of years old and the most ancient text of Jewish meditation, instructs us, "Bridle your mouth from speaking and your heart from thinking. And if your heart runs, return to the Place." When you can come to internal silence, you will grasp the words of the Psalmist—"Silence is your greatest praise" (Psalm 65)—and be filled with great joy.

The Jewish prayer book reminds us, "Even if our mouths were filled with song as the sea is filled with water, our tongue with melody as the roar of the waves, and our lips with praise as the breath of the firmament, and our eyes were radiant as the sun and moon . . . ," we would not have words adequate to praise and thank God. At a certain point during prayer, we realize that words only block the experience of intimacy with the Creator, which cannot be conceptualized in words. Just like a lover wants to gaze or kiss the beloved when there are no words adequate to express a love that is beyond words, the silence of meditation provides the soul the opportunity to cling to God in the most direct way. Meditation is the experience of an intimacy with the Creator that cannot be articulated in words. At the deepest level of truth, there are no words to talk about God for He is beyond words, no thoughts to think for He is beyond thought. Prayer and meditation are intertwined like the inhalation and exhalation of the breath. Heartfelt prayer lifts us to the place beyond words, a place of intimacy, the place of meditation. The silence experienced in meditation again gives rise to words of prayer because we tend to articulate our experiences in language.

TOUCHING INFINITY

The goal of *New Age Judaism* is to expand our consciousness of ourselves and of God. The following powerful meditation has been adapted and simplified from *Sefer Yetzirah*. The meditation demonstrates many of the basics that have been presented about God. I believe that this meditation helps to further free us of the limiting anthropomorphic images we have of God and to open us even more to the new spiritual paradigm of the New Age. This powerful meditation guides us on an imaginative journey in which we gaze into the realm of infinity, where time and space are unlimited and boundless. It demonstrates experientially many of the basic things we have been learning about God. Through this meditation, we may clearly experience that we are in the center of God. This is a wonderful awareness. Though best done in a sitting position, I also like to do an abridged version of this meditation when I am walking outside.

 Meditation on Touching Infinity

Assume a comfortable seated position and center yourself with your breath. Allow your mind to travel to back in time ten years. Take a breath. Now imagine you can travel back fifty years, though you may not have been born then. Now imagine you can go back a hundred years, then a thousand years, then two thousand years, then five thousand years and so forth. Keep going back farther and farther. Go as far as you can imagine. When you are unable to go farther, when "farther" is beyond your powers of imagination, you have touched infinity. Know and respect that there is a realm in time, before even time was created, that you cannot enter. Slowly bring your awareness to the present moment and take a few deep breaths.

Now allow your mind to travel into the future. Go forward in time. Imagine the world in ten years, in a hundred years, in a thousand years. And then ten thousand years. Know that you can go farther and farther, until you arrive at a place where you can go no farther. Your mind can conceive no farther. This is infinity. Then slowly bring your awareness to the present moment and take a few deep breaths.

Now allow your mind to travel through space going upward. Imagine traveling through the heavens, past the stars, leaving this galaxy, traveling into other galaxies and going upward and upward until you arrive at a place where you can go no farther. Again you have hit infinity. Slowly bring your awareness back to the present moment and the present space and take a few deep breaths.

Now imagine that you can travel downward, into the earth, and then again into space, going downward. Keep going, through the galaxies, until you can go no farther, for you have hit infinity.

Now imagine that you can travel to the north, traveling in the northern direction as far as you can conceive. Keep going northward until you can go no farther in your imagination for you have again hit infinity. Slowly return your awareness to the present moment, the place where you are.

Now imagine that you can travel to the south. Keep going south from wherever you are, going more and more to the south until you can no longer conceive journeying any farther in your imagination. You have again hit infinity. Slowly bring your awareness to the present moment, your present place.

Imagine that you can travel to the east. Keep going eastward in your imagination as far as possible. Keep going until you hit infinity. Now travel back to the present moment, the present place.

Imagine that you travel west. Keep going westward in your imagination as far as possible. Keep going westward until you again hit infinity, until you cannot conceive of anything farther west. Slowly bring your awareness back to the present moment and the present place.

Take a few deep breaths and breathe in the awareness that you are sitting in the middle of infinity. You are a part of this infinity. You are in the center of infinity. Every point in infinity is the center. Infinity is the best metaphor for God. Kabbalah uses the term *Ain Sof,* "without limit," for what we normally call "God." God is infinite.

God surrounds Creation. Yet God is also within this world because this world is within God. You are in God, and God is within you. Wherever you are, you are within God. Everything occurs within Him. You are in the middle of God. God is called the *Makom,* the "Place of the World," because everything is within Him. You are in the *Makom.* You are in the Place of God.

Wherever you are, God is with you. Sit silently in the awareness of the presence of infinity, in the presence of God. Wherever you are, whoever you are, you are in the center of God. Breathe this awareness in and, as you exhale, let go. Allow the walls that you have constructed, that separate you from this awareness, to be relaxed. Transcend your identification with the limited personality and the ego self. You are not alone or on your own. With each breath, let go, open, expand and connect to what is beyond you. Be permeated by this awareness. Be rooted in this awareness. Continue to take deep breaths. In kabbalah this infinity is called *Or Ain Sof,* "Limitless Light." Sit in the awareness of infinite light. Let this light enter you and permeate you on all levels of being: physically, emotionally and spiritually.

Imagine you can breathe with your whole physical body. Your entire body opens, expands and contracts. Your organs breathe. Everything within you pulsates. Everything opens, reaches toward infinity and then contracts. Your physical body is surrounded by an astral body. Imagine that this astral body expands in all directions. Imagine that your emotional body can also breathe and that you can now vibrate your feelings. If you would like, become aware of a hurt that you have held deep inside. Breathe it out toward infinity. Let it go. Give it to the light. Light dissolves negativity, light dispels darkness. Let light into the spaces where this hurt resided. Continue to open. Now imagine that your soul can breathe. Feel the soul's deep desire to expand, to leave the confines of the physical body, to merge with the Infinite One. Then feel the soul's desire to return to the physical body and feel the joy of being in a physical body. Expand and contract. Experience opening and letting go.

Continue to open to the expanded awareness of infinity. You are free to expand your consciousness as much as you can. You are free to contract your consciousness as much as you want. This is your choice. However, wherever you are, wherever you go—to the highest place, to the lowest place—you are always in the middle of infinity. There is no place else to go. There is no place to hide. Because infinity contains within it that which is finite, every point within infinity is the center. You are the center point in the middle of infinity.

2

THE ONENESS OF GOD

Several times each day for thousands of years, observant Jews have been saying the *Shema*, which is *"Shema Yisrael, Adonoy Eloheynu, Adonoy Echod."* This means "Hear, O Israel, the Lord your God, the Lord is One." These very words have traditionally been the last words said by martyrs and saints. The *Shema* is the most basic affirmation of Judaism. These words sum up the profundity of what the Jewish tradition knows about God. In these six simple words, God tells us who He is. God is one. Interestingly enough, the *Shema* instructs us to hear, to listen. We are told that we need to listen if we are to know God's oneness. God tells us to listen. Listening is a call to quiet the mind so that we can truly hear, so that we can know and understand. Within the simplicity of the *Shema* are found the deepest secrets of the universe. It is the most powerful teaching, and if understood and experienced it will transform your life. The *Shema* is the key to the unity consciousness of the New Age.

If we are to understand the depths of the *Shema* with our whole being, we must understand intellectually what we mean when we say "God is one." Most people will say that the *Shema* means that there is only one God, which means that everything was created by

15

this one God. This is true and is itself an important and profound teaching. Your race and your religion do not matter. We are all created by this same unknowable, powerful and awesome God, and as such we all have an equal right to be alive. Sadly, I meet people who do not feel that way or even that they are entitled to be alive. They feel that there is no place for them in this world. Often they received these messages directly or indirectly early in their lives from their parents. They did not feel wanted by their parents and felt that their very existence was a terrible burden. The *Shema* powerfully affirms personal worth. "I am created by God." This is a wonderful affirmation to repeat over and over. And the *Shema* is deeper than this.

The second commandment is "You shall have no other gods before Me." The Talmud says, "Whoever denies idolatry, it is as if he fulfilled the whole Torah." A *midrash,* a story in the Jewish oral tradition, tells that Abraham, considered to be the first Jew and the father of the Jewish people, destroyed the idols of his father and then left one idol and put an ax in its hand. When his father confronted him about the destruction of the idols—selling idols was his father's business—Abraham blamed the remaining idol for destroying the others. Of course, Abraham was being facetious to make his point.

In ancient times, people worshipped the sun and moon as intermediaries to God because they did not feel worthy of approaching the awesome and invisible God directly. They needed something they could see or touch to serve as a go-between, to help focus their awareness. Soon they forgot that the original intention of idolatry was to worship the one God. They then created idols, large and small that had powers over different forces in nature. There was the fertility goddess, the war god, the agriculture god and so on. People became more and more confused and began to worship the idols they made. People had to go to one idol to pray for one thing and to another for something else. If one idol did not deliver what was wanted, they could attempt to appease another one. This kept the ancients very busy. The ancient world was filled with many gods and goddesses who were made in the image of man. These gods and goddesses were human in temperament and even had sexual consorts. Sexual promiscuity was also often associated, quite conveniently, in many pagan rites with idol worship.

Even though idolatry is prevalent in some current spiritual practices, most people today do not bow down to idols of stone, wood or gold as they did thousands of years ago. Yet idolatry in a larger sense is still prevalent in more subtle forms in modern secular society. Idolatry occurs whenever we transfer our personal power to objects or forces other than God. For example, it is a form of idolatry when we transfer our power to the modern idols of power, wealth and fame, and feel that we must serve them to solidify our own identities. All too often we place our faith in what we have created, in what we can see, touch or feel, and not in God. We proclaim that what we think, feel and do are the source of what happens in our lives, that we are the ones who make things happen. When we put our leaders, our teachers and even our lovers on pedestals, follow them blindly, and refuse to see who they really are, this is a form of idolatry. It is also a subtle form of idolatry to see others as things to be exploited for our personal gain.

We can even idolize ourselves. When we form an image of ourselves that we feel we must live up to, even if it is not congruent with our experience of who we are, this is also a subtle form of idolatry. We can even idolize God. Many people treat their concept of God as an idol, much as people worshipped idols in ancient times. They try to appease God with prayers and actions. We may say that we believe in God, but often it is only what we want or think God should be that we believe in. We want God on our terms, and for many that is merely a more romanticized or improved version of themselves: God should be everything we want Him to be or we do not believe in Him. He should protect and love us. He should be good to us. It is popular to say that "God is love." That is a Christian concept. The Torah says, "God does good, and creates evil." God in Judaism is not something sweet and sentimental but rather the underlying reality that encompasses good and bad.

When we reflect on the expanded definition of idolatry, we can see that Judaism's message against idolatry is still very relevant today. In the Bible, God continually expresses His anger about the Jews' fascination with the idols of the surrounding cultures. At first glance, it appears that God is jealous: He wants the Jews to give Him their undivided love and worship. If we consider the matter more deeply, we can appreciate that it is for our sake that God wants us to leave idolatry. If our sense of self is externally determined, we are alienated from our true selves and from God, living an artificial reality in which we give our power to things that we have created rather than attach ourselves to the source of all Creation, the True Reality. This is, in essence, a disempowering and limiting process that makes us vulnerable to the forces of evil. To see how this manifests, we have only to look at how totalitarian governments feast on individuals who give away their power. If we feel unsteady or depressed, often it is because we placed our trust in forces other than God. To make a connection with God, we have to let go of our artificial concepts of who God is and who we are and call out to Him from the depths of our souls.

Monotheism, the primary Jewish spiritual contribution to the world, is more than the negation of idolatry. The *Shema* means much more than that there is one God as opposed to many gods. Rather, it expresses the belief in the unity of God. When we say "God is one," we mean that God cannot be divided into parts. It also means that God is unique. If God had parts, He would not be one. We say, therefore, that God is a unity. God is whole. God is one.

FREE WILL VERSUS DIVINE PROVIDENCE

When we say that God is one we are saying that in actuality, in essence and in truth everything flows from God and is part of God. The good comes from God and the not so good also comes from God. There is only one force in the world, and that is God. One of the most difficult concepts to grasp in Judaism is that we are both inseparably part of God and free to exercise our personal will. The Bible says, "I have set before thee this day life and good, and death and evil. . . . therefore choose life" (Deut. 30:19). The Bible also says, "I form light and create darkness: I make peace and create evil" (Isa. 45:7).

Does God make things happen or do we? If humans have free will, how can we say that everything is God's Will? Judaism says that both are true. There is free will and there is Divine Providence. This is complex and difficult to understand. From the Jewish perspective, we are told that we have free will and that we create our reality to a large extent and yet, paradoxically, that what happens to us is Divine Will. We are also told there is no such thing as coincidence. How then, in light of God's mercy, when we are told that God created this world to bestow goodness, do we explain suffering? Is it Divine Will that we suffer? (We will explore this question of suffering in much greater depth in chapter 8.)

According to Rabbi Moses Luzzatto in his classic book *The Way of God,* God in His power could have created a perfect world but in His wisdom chose not to do so. If the world was perfect, what meaning would our actions have? He could have made us perfect, but would we feel good about ourselves? What would our perfection mean if we did not earn it? We earn our perfection through our free will. We are given a *yetzer tov,* a good inclination, and we are also given a *yetzer hara,* an evil urge. Both inclinations are balanced so that we are not compelled toward either of them. Our life is often a battleground between these two internal inclinations. God created this challenge for us because we grow and become refined through challenge. By our own choices, we exercise our free will to perfect ourselves—and the world. We have to work hard to gain self-mastery over our thoughts, our speech and our actions. It is not easy, because we are pulled in many directions. We feel better about our accomplishments when we have had to work for them and what we achieve has more meaning and value to us and possibly to God. Though we have a tendency to blame God when we suffer, the deeper truth is that God is loving and we are not innocent victims. It is we who bear the consequences of our actions, feelings and thoughts. We cannot be passive and say it is God's Will that we suffer.

On the other hand, according to Bachya Ibn Paquda, author of one of my favorite books, *Duties of the Heart,* no one hurts anyone without God's permission. Nothing happens randomly. Everything is Divine Providence. Everything has purpose. A person is advised to see the events of his or her life and those occurring in the world not as coincidental but as emanating from God. We do this not to experience ourselves as victims of divine punishment but to be able to extract the goodness in whatever is happening to us, and thus to become better and more noble people.

Ibn Paquda told us that the questions of good and evil diminish as we grow in spiritual awareness. He provided the following analogy: If we have weak eyes and cannot enjoy the light of the sun, we have to wear a thin veil to protect our eyes. The more impaired our eyes, the thicker the veil needed to protect them. As our eyes improve, the veil may become thinner.

As we purify ourselves, we become ready and worthy to experience God's light with fewer veils. With God's Light we are able to see the Divine Goodness in everything that happens, and we glimpse God's oneness underlying the vast array of life experiences. This opens us to the deepest love and joy, and even to ecstasy. We were created to experience this joy. Those who affirm God's oneness and trust in Him enjoy a deep sense of tranquillity regardless of whatever happens because they see that everything emanates from God. Such people enjoy divine intimacy, protection and revelation.

THE ULTIMATE PARADOX

Within the simple words of the *Shema,* "Hear O Israel, the Lord your God, the Lord is One," lies the deepest paradox. The *Shema* affirms that God is both transcendent and immanent. The first time we say God's name in the *Shema,* we are meditating on the transcendence of God. God is outside and greater than Creation, God is an other, a Being we can never know. The second time we are meditating on the immanence of God. God is within Creation, animating and sustaining all forms of life.

How can one God be outside of Creation and equally within Creation and still be a unified whole? This is the ultimate spiritual paradox and the deepest question. Does not the world make a difference to God? Is God's unity disturbed by the creation of the world? In the prophet Malachi, we read, "I, the Lord, have not changed." In the classic book of Lubavitch Chassidus, *Tanya,* the Alter Rebbe, the founder of the Lubavitch movement, explained how we can say that God is not changed by Creation. Just as we say that God was unique, alone and single before Creation, we say the same things about Him after Creation, because everything created is as nothing in comparison to Him.

In a section of *Tanya*, Shaar Hayichud (Gate of Unity), the Alter Rebbe provided the following illustration to explain this idea: Compare the light of the sun to the sun itself. The light may spread a great distance, but what is it in relation to the sun? The light is a part of the sun and has no existence by itself. So similarly we are nothing in relation to God. If I feel that I am a ray of God's Light, I experience oneness with God. We may like to think that we are independent of God but, in the deepest truth, we are not.

The Alter Rebbe went on to say that all the worlds, and there are more worlds than this one physical world, were created by the speech of God. He gave the analogy of a person who speaks: The actual words are absolutely nothing in comparison to his faculty for speech. The Bible describes Creation as a series of utterances: "And God spoke." Why does the Bible use the metaphor of human speech to describe what happens at Creation? Why not action or thought when man in Judaism is said to create on three basic levels: thought, speech and action?

Rabbi Simon Jacobson explained that speech is used to describe Creation because what is spoken exists, yet it does not have an independent existence. If the Torah had used the metaphor of thought, and God only thought the world, the world would not appear to have a separate existence. What we think remains internal. If the Torah had said God made the world, the world would be separate from Him. Whatever we make, once it is made, it is separate from us. Speech is the perfect metaphor because it depends on the speaker speaking. If the speaker ceases to speak, there is no speech. By using the metaphor of speech, the Bible tells us that God is constantly creating everything anew and that everything in existence is in essence a divine communication. Similarly we and our world seem to have a sense of existence, but we do not exist independent of God. We are only God's speech.

These ideas may be challenging, for we like to think that we are in control of our lives, we take pride in making things happen, and we judge ourselves and others harshly when things do not happen as we want. But how substantial are we really? We have to acknowledge that many things happen that are beyond our control, and ultimately, whether we like it or not, we will age and we will die. The essence of Judaism, manifest in all its laws and requirements, is to purify and refine people so as to enable them to realize that God is the source, God is the essence of life. To know this requires surrender on our part.

Abraham's first instructions from God, as reported in the Torah portion named Lech Lecha, which interestingly enough means "Go to Yourself," are "Leave your land, your family, and your father's house to the land I will show you." God tells him to leave, but He does not tell him where to go. This was a test that made Abraham truly worthy of entering into divine service. It was a test because there was no clarity. Abraham had to let go of all the attachments that had shaped his sense of self and to be in a state of not knowing. This took great faith. The rabbis tell us that whatever happened to the forefathers and foremothers, as recorded in the Torah, will happen to us to a lesser extent as individuals and as members of the Jewish people. The patriarchs and matriarchs serve as role models for us. From Abraham we learn that if we truly want to come close to God we, too, must let go of our egos and physical attachments, trust our inner voices even when they don't make sense, and find the natural divine faith within us to go forward. When we have no clarity of purpose when confronted with the situations life presents us, we should ask "What does God want?" and listen deeply inside. Quiet the mind and meditate, for we cannot hear the "I" of God if our egos are talking.

The Baal Shem Tov said that the highest gates to meditation are open only to those who are indifferent to praise or insult. We must have a detachment from the ego. If we prefer praise over insult, this indicates that we have not reached the higher levels of God-connection. We become more humble, less concerned with honor for self, upon coming closer to God. Humility is close to Godliness. The greatest Jewish prophet, Moses, who led the Jewish people out of Egypt and spoke directly to God, was said to be the most humble person. Humility and greatness go together in Judaism because truly great people can easily surrender their egos to God. Those with low self-esteem will not be able to relinquish the selves they do not feel good about. Such people must build the self up slowly by attaching to God. When they feel good about themselves and their egos are stronger, they will be better able to surrender themselves to God.

As we grow spiritually by clinging to God, it becomes easier to shed old and limiting ways of experiencing self. All growth requires a certain degree of *bittul,* which is the Hebrew word for "nothingness." Just as a seed has to rot before it becomes a plant, so similarly, we have to suspend limiting ideas of self in order to allow something greater to come through us. It is only through self-nullification, through surrender, that a person may experience the oneness of God. That cannot be fully experienced if a person's ego is also present. *Bittul* is the highest state of spiritual awareness and requires much purification, effort and grace. Rabbi Nachman said that it is impossible to attain the state of *bittul* without meditation. By secluding ourselves, expressing ourselves directly to God, we can nullify our negative traits and transcend the ego and physicality. During such times, we recognize that we are not our egos, not our bodies, not our feelings, that we do not have any real existence, and that ultimately there is only God. Through intense love, devotion and dedication to spiritual practices, we *bittul* (nullify) ourselves and let go of a limited sense of ego and physical self. Yet the recognition of this nothingness, this nonexistence, does not lower self-esteem but rather fills us with a great joy, bringing about the experience of a deep sense of unity with everything in Creation. We can experience ourselves as a part of God. We feel like a drop of water in the ocean, yet we taste the whole ocean for the whole ocean is contained in that drop. God is eternal. When we are in a state of *bittul,* time seems to stop and we spend more time in a sense of eternity. As God is eternal, so we taste eternity in each passing moment.

The *Shema* is our ticket to the highest spiritual awareness of *bittul.* It contains all the secrets within it. When we say the *Shema,* we customarily close our eyes because God is first found in the inner depths of our own soul. As Reb Shlomo Carlebach said, "God is closer to us than our own breath." If something is far away from us, we generally have to open our eyes wide to see it. If something is close to us, we can relax our gaze. If something is very close to us, we can close our eyes because we can sense its presence. When we say the *Shema* we proclaim God's oneness, yet to truly experience His oneness is a great spiritual achievement and blessing. Do not be discouraged as we may spend our whole lifetime praying, meditating, learning and living a pure and holy life only to have a few precious moments when we truly understand, on all levels of our being, what God's oneness is.

Judaism teaches that there is the experience of the higher unity of God and the experience of the lower unity. When we say the *Shema* we affirm the higher unity of God; that is, everything is God. In the words of Moses, "There is nothing but God." God is one, and everything is a part of God. There is only God. There is no world, there is no self, only God. God is the ultimate and true reality and everything is a manifestation of the divine. This is the greatest joy. To experience oneness with another person is a great joy. To experience oneness with God is ecstasy.

As physical and human beings, it is not our fate to remain in the spiritual world of unity. God created a world of differentiation, and we have to return to the physical world with its multiplicity of forms. The experience of oneness, whether it is with another person or with God, lasts a brief time, yet we are changed irrevocably through it. We move close, we merge and then we separate. This is the dance of life. Kabbalah calls it "running and returning." We ascend to the spiritual world, then we return to the physical world. This is our destiny as human beings. And so it is that after we say the *Shema* we express the lower unity of God and say in a whisper, "Blessed is the name of your glorious kingdom forever and ever." We then open our eyes, and look to see God in the multiformity of life. Now we are aware that we exist, as does everyone else, and that this is God's world and that God is King of this world.

Meditation on the *Shema*

Take a moment to experience the concepts we have been discussing by saying the *Shema* in a meditative way.

Begin by taking a few deep breaths. Breathe from the abdomen to the rib cage to the chest and exhale through the mouth, making a sound like a wave in the ocean. Do this several times until you feel yourself relaxed and centered. We prepare to say the *Shema* by first working on the letters of the *Shema: shin, mem* and *aleph.* We substitute the *aleph* for the *ayin* because the *shin,* the *mem* and the *aleph* are the "mother" letters of the Hebrew alphabet. According to kabbalah, Creation occurred through words, which are composed of letters, and thus the Hebrew letters contain powerful energies. If you do not know the Hebrew letters, you can still do this exercise, as you will be guided to visualize the color and make the sound associated with each letter.

Visualize the *shin* in your head, in orange light. The *shin* represents the element of fire. You can almost see the flames of fire in its shape. Picture the *shin,* take a deep breath and, on the exhalation, make the sound of the *shin,* "shhhhhh," extending it for the entire exhalation.

Now visualize the *mem* in your solar plexus, in blue light. The *mem* represents the element of water, bringing harmony to all levels of being. Continue visualizing the *mem,* take a deep breath and, on the exhalation, make the sound of the *mem,* "mmmmmmm," extending it for the entire exhalation.

Now visualize the *aleph* a few inches above the top of your head, in white light. The *aleph* represents the element of air. The *aleph* connects us to *Ain Sof,* God's Light before Creation. The *aleph* is silent.

Repeat the meditation on these letters at least three more times, each time allowing the letters to go deep inside.

When you say the *shin* for the fourth time, visualize yourself in the midst of holy fire. When you say the *mem,* visualize that you are immersed in the depths of water. When you see the *aleph,* visualize yourself floating in air. Repeat this visualization several times.

Now you will chant each word of the *Shema* as you did the Hebrew letters. With each exhalation, chant each word of the *Shema.* When saying God's name—*Adonoy*—for the first time, visualize the letters of the Divine Name—*Yud Hay Vav Hay*—before you on your inner screen, the space in front of you when your eyes are closed, and be aware that God is transcendent, outside of Creation. When you say God's name the second time, place the letters of the Divine Name inside of you. Visualize the *yud* in your head, the *hay* in your shoulders and arms, the *vav* in your torso, and the final *hay* in your waist and legs. Be aware that God is immanent. God is within Creation. When you say the last word of the *Shema, Echod,* be aware that God fills this universe, His presence pervades the six directions: north, south, east, west, up and down.

Chant the *Shema* with the *kavannot* (contemplations) prescribed above. With each exhalation, say another word. *"Shema . . . Yisrael . . . Adonoy . . . Eloheynu . . . Adonoy . . . Echod."* "Hear, O Israel, the Lord your God, the Lord is One." Listen. . . . God is transcendent. . . . God is immanent. . . . God is a unity. Everything flows out of His oneness. In a whisper, say the next line of the *Shema: "Baruch shem kvod malchuto l'olam va-ed."* "Blessed is the name of His glorious kingdom for all eternity."

When we say the *Shema* we are meditating to access the faith within us that unifies everything that happens in our life. Take a moment to reflect on the events of the day or recent events, imagine that everything is a message, a communication from God. There is something to learn about yourself through each person and event you have encountered.

3

THE HOW AND WHY OF CREATION

Most of us have wondered at some time how this physical world was created and why it was created as it was. We have wondered why we were born and what a human being is. We sense we are more than physical beings, but who are we really? Where do we come from? Is this physical world the only world that exists? We say God is in heaven. Where is heaven? When we die, do we go to heaven? Is heaven up in the sky somewhere? These deep questions are the subject matter of kabbalah. Please remember that kabbalah is not the product of human reasoning. It is not rational but mystical. As we come to understand more about the mystery of Creation, we also understand ourselves better, for we are a part of this mystery.

The deepest teachings about why and how Creation actually occurred are recorded in detail in a kabbalistic book entitled *Etz Hayim*, or *Tree of Life*. These are the teachings of Rabbi Yitzchok Luria, also known as the Arizel, who claimed to receive them from the Prophet Elijah. These teachings are considered the holiest and deepest teachings of kabbalah. As originally written, these teachings are abstract and hard to understand. I present a simplification of them here. These teachings constitute the map of reality that, when understood, elevates and helps us in very practical ways (see chapter 4).

Etz Hayim begins by telling us that there arose within God, who is called *Ain Sof,* the will, the desire, to create a world that He could love and be known by. *Ain Sof* then did what is known as *tzimtzum* to Himself; that is, *Ain Sof* contracted Himself to create space for Creation to occur within Him. It was a decisive action resembling the big bang theory of Creation. The contraction began in the center of *Ain Sof.* Because *Ain Sof* is infinite, the center was wherever the point of Creation was. The Light of *Ain Sof* was withdrawn and reentered the void in a lesser and more differentiated expression than before—enough light to sustain Creation but not too much to obliterate it. Too much light would have nullified Creation and returned it to pre-Creation existence. How does infinite light pervade what is not infinite? How does God coexist with His Creation and not overwhelm it? This is the ultimate paradox, yet this is what happened. Creation must become independent of God to exist, yet all that is created cannot exist if it is not connected and part of God.

Etz Hayim goes on to say that *Ain Sof* unfolded worlds one from another. As the worlds were unfolded downward, the *tzimtzum* became greater and the holiness, the Light of *Ain Sof,* became more encased in "garments," in the words of the Arizel. Four worlds were created within this contracted space. Each of these worlds has a distinct character. Only our world is physical, bound by the constraints of time and space. The other worlds are spiritual in nature. Though these spiritual worlds have their own realities, which are beyond us, they are also reflected in our world—and even within ourselves. Because of this, we can glimpse their existence and have some understanding of them.

The first world created is called *Atzilut. Atzilut* is derived from the root *etzel,* meaning "nearness." This is because *Atzilut* is closest to *Ain Sof. Atzilut* is still so close to *Ain Sof* that it is fully absorbed in it. This is a world of spiritual unity. It is the domain where the *sephirot,* the Divine Emanations, become differentiated. The *sephirot* are the circular and linear channels by which the Light of *Ain Sof* interacts with the worlds He created. We actually experience God through the *sephirot.* Though the *sephirot* are not *Ain Sof* and we are cautioned not to pray to them as if they were God, they are the vehicles and filters for God's Light. (We will learn more about the *sephirot* in the next chapter.)

On the level of human experience, the world of *Atzilut* is our superconsciousness. It is the levels of our soul known as *yehida* and *chaya* where we experience ourselves as a part of God. These levels of soul are outside the physical body. The world of *Atzilut* is reflected within us in a deep sense of being, where the "I am" of God resounds. This is the world we glimpse when we say the *Shema*.

The next world created by *Ain Sof* is called *Beriyah*, "Creation," which is below *Atzilut*. The name *Beriyah* comes from the word *bara*, which means "to create." The world of *Beriyah* is separate and outside the direct realm of *Ain Sof*. In this context, Creation means "something from nothing." *Beriyah* is also called the "Universe of the Throne" because it is said that God "sits" here, which means that He lowers His essence to be available to Creation. Our prayers ascend to the world of Beriyah. The archangels Michael, Gabriel, Raphael and Uriel reside there.

On the level of our human experience, the world of *Beriyah* is the level of the higher mind, the witness consciousness. It is the level of soul known as *neshama*. The seat of *neshama* is located at the top of the head. On this level, we experience ourselves as separate enough from God that we can perceive and think about Him.

The next world *Ain Sof* created is called *Yetzirah*. This term comes from the root *yatzar*, meaning "to form." In kabbalah, "forming" means to take something that exists and give it new shape. *Yetzirah* is primarily the world of angels who are the spiritual forces closest to our physical world and available to us. On the level of our human experience, this world is the heart, the world of feelings and emotions. The heart is the central organ in our bodies, pumping the blood throughout our bodies, and it is the seat of the level of soul known as *ruach*. The heart is the place of yearning. Like the angels who are messengers of divine blessing, so also is our heart the juice, the vehicle for the transportation of our thoughts to physical manifestation.

The fourth world is known as *Assiyah*. *Assiyah* is the world of "making," coming from the root word *Oseh*. *Assiyah* is our world of physicality, yet it is not devoid of spirituality. Our world is both physical and spiritual, and everything within this world has a body and soul. The world of *Assiyah* is the world of action. What we do or do not do makes a difference in this world. We have to work, we have to meet our physical needs, we have to choose, we have to act. Even our choice not to act is an action. What we do and what we do not do have consequences—and not only for ourselves. The world of *Assiyah* corresponds to the level of soul known as *nefesh*. It is this soul energy that empowers the body to function, giving our eyes the power to see, our ears the power to hear, and so forth. (It is said that the *nefesh* of a person stays with the body even after death.)

The How and Why of Creation

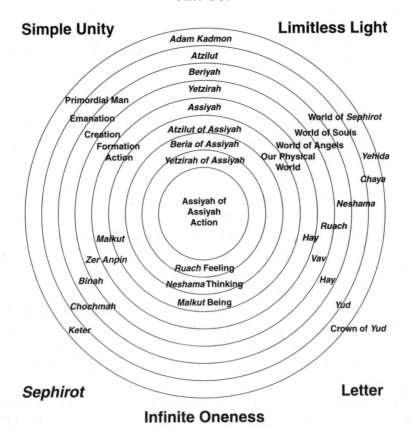

All the spiritual worlds are contained within our world of *Assiyah*. We tend to think that the spiritual is higher than the material. We take this literally, and we look to heaven. We look upward to find God because we need to raise our consciousness to see God, but God is not in heaven, though He is there, too. God is within. What kabbalah says is that the spiritual is actually deeper, more inner, at the core of everything. To find God we need to look inward. We need to go beyond appearances and beyond physicality to penetrate to the essence of things.

The essence of everything is spiritual. Interestingly enough, modern science tells us that everything in our world is composed of various configurations of atoms, neutrons, protons and other microscopic particles surrounded by space. Things appear to be solid, but they are not. Einstein's famous theory, $E=mc^2$, revolutionized our understanding of the physical world. It was a breakthrough idea but one in accordance with kabbalah and Judaism. Though I am neither scientifically oriented nor knowledgeable, I understand that the essence of Einstein's theory was that everything is energy. Matter can be converted to energy. Energy can be converted to matter. We have learned how to convert matter into energy. When we do so, it unleashes awesome power. For example, atomic power and nuclear power are both matter converted to energy. In fact, matter is a very powerful, more concentrated form of energy. Matter appears to be solid, but it is essentially energy resonating at clearly defined frequencies.

The physical world is a condensation of spiritual energy, and as such it has the potential to contain more Divine Light than the spiritual worlds that are only spiritual in essence. Though the physical world is the world farthest away from *Ain Sof*, it is said in kabbalah that our physical world of *Assiyah* is the purpose of all of Creation and that all worlds are created to serve our physical world. All the spiritual worlds are contained within our world, and our world is contained within all the other worlds. We cannot see the space that is in everything, but let's consider that God is the space within and God is the space surrounding all things. God is the force, the energy, the consciousness that gives all life existence. God is the deepest, the most pure essence. God is everywhere. Nothing can exist independently of God. To find God, we simply have to perceive the spiritual essence of things, of people, of ourselves. With the right eyes, we can see God everywhere because God is at the center of everything.

According to kabbalah, the original prototype for the Creation of the world is vessels and lights. Though the vessels themselves are also light, they are more dense in comparison to the light they contain, so they are called vessels. God created vessels of varying densities to contain and reflect Divine Light. Everything is a vessel for light. Even light can be a vessel for a higher, more refined light.

Light has always been the closest metaphor kabbalah has for the divine influence. The desire for spiritual light is at the heart of all our desires, whether we know it or not. Kabbalah has many names for spiritual light: holy light, hidden light, inner light, surrounding light and more. Kabbalists would meditate on the light of the Divine Presence and experience ecstasy. Rebbes would see "from one corner of the world to another" with spiritual light. Envisioning God as light is also popular in New Age meditations. Because spiritual light is impersonal and its nature is to radiate everywhere, opening to spiritual light in meditation is liberating, particularly to those who have felt trapped in the old spiritual paradigm. Meditations on spiritual light provide a most immediate taste of the Divine Presence.

The most important questions to ask ourselves in meditation and in life are these: "Am I open to receive and radiate God's Light?" "Am I the proper vessel to receive God's Light?" "How do I bring God's Light into all the vessels that compose my life?" "How do I bring God's Light into places in darkness in this world that call out for light?" It would be very worthwhile to sit with each of these questions from time to time, as well as to ask these questions while going about the daily business of life. Breathe, open and reflect.

Remember that we each have many desires, but unless we are open, unless we are vessels to allow what we desire into our life, we will not have what we want. As much as we want, we do not know how to receive. We are often afraid to receive what we want. Learning how to receive and how to be a proper vessel is a very important capacity acquired through meditation.

Take a moment to consider how everything, every person, every event is a vessel for God's Light. Affirm these words to yourself in meditation: "My body is a vessel for my soul." "My work is a vessel for my love." This is the truth. View your problems as vessels for your spiritual growth. They simply inform you of the blockages within you that you need to open so God's Light can enter. Right now, take a meditation break. Take a few deep breaths. Repeat one of the above affirmations, reflect and see if your heart does not fill with gratitude.

When we perceive everything in our lives as a vessel for the Light of *Ain Sof,* we are able to extract the Divine Light in whatever is happening to us. This is spiritually nourishing and transformational. When we do this, God's Light flows through us with greater intensity. As we welcome God's Light within us and see God's Light in everything, we are better able to let go of the obstacles of the ego mind that impede the flow of Divine Light. We are happier. When we fail to do this and experience materialism as an end in itself, we become disconnected from God's Light. We feel like victims. This is the root of suffering and evil.

The following charts will help you begin to see clearly how kabbalah makes connections between levels of soul, spiritual worlds and parts of the body. These connections form the basis for meditative kabbalah. The letters of the Divine Name are the wings, and the name is a chariot for travel. Meditating on the letters of the Divine Name is a form of invocation. Just as we respond when our name is called, so does God. At the conclusion of this chapter, you will find basic and powerful meditations to give you a taste of what has been described above.

World	Level of Soul	Letter of Divine Name
Adam kadmon (will)	*Yehida*	Crown of *Yud*
Atzilut (nearness)	*Chaya*	*Yud*
Beriyah (Creation)	*Neshama*	*Hay*
Yetzirah (formation)	*Ruach*	*Vav*
Assiyah (action)	*Nefesh*	*Hay*

World	Level of Soul	Letter of Divine Name
Yehida	Most Inner Essence	Crown of *Yud*
Chaya	Aura (outside the body)	*Yud*
Neshama	Mind (thinking, head)	*Hay*
Yetzirah	Heart (feeling, torso)	*Vav*
Assiyah	Action (doing, legs)	*Hay*

SUPPLEMENTARY KABBALISTIC MEDITATIONS

 ## Meditation on Being a Vessel for *Ain Sof*

Take a few deep breaths, breathing in and out through the nostrils. With each inhalation, feel the joy and gift of each breath. With each exhalation, allow yourself to go deeper inside. Allow the mind to quiet as you focus on the breath. Continue to follow the breath inside. Pause in the spaces between the breaths, where the exhalation ends and before the new inhalation begins. Pause again when the inhalation ends and before the exhalation begins. Allow your consciousness to roam in the quiet and empty place between the breaths. Feel the desire for a new breath, and the desire to give way to the exhalation. Sit with your breathing for a few minutes, continuing to quiet the mind as you focus on the breath.

Imagine that you can travel back in time, to the place before time and space were created. Before there was what we know as the beginning, there was only *Ain Sof*. It is said that there arose a desire within *Ain Sof* to give and to be known. As there was only *Ain Sof,* there was nothing to give to and nothing to be known by. *Ain Sof* could not be known as compassionate, forgiving or patient if there was no Creation. He could not be known as YHVH, the name that indicates He is forever, if there were no time, no past, no present and no future. Something other than *Ain Sof* needed to exist for *Ain Sof* to experience Himself in these ways. Interestingly enough, the desire to give and to be known are the deepest desires within us as well. Much like *Ain Sof,* the desires to give love and to be known underlie our thoughts, desires and actions.

Take a few deep breaths. With each breath that gives you life, be aware of the desire that *Ain Sof* had to create this world. *Ain Sof* desired to create you. Allow yourself to open and expand with each breath. *Ain Sof,* God, created this world to bestow goodness and to be known. This goodness, this knowledge, is available to us if we open to it. With each breath open like a vessel. Continue to expand and let go with each deep breath. Allow yourself to become empty. Experience yourself as an empty vessel. Feel your yearning to be filled with Godliness. Know that it was for this reason you were created. You were created to be a vessel for Godliness. Imagine yourself in a column of light and love. This light surrounds and permeates you.

Sit in meditation for as long as you like.

 ## Meditation on the Holy Soul

Experiencing the divinity of your own soul is a most important and basic awareness for the New Age paradigm. This is who you really are.

The following is an intermediate-level meditation practice for those who have meditation experience. It is not essential that you know the Hebrew letters for this meditation, but it is helpful.

Take a few deep breaths to center yourself. Inhale deeply through the abdomen and exhale slowly through the mouth. Do this for a few minutes until you feel relaxed and focused. "God breathes into you a pure soul." Repeat this silently to yourself a few times. Feel your identity as this pure soul. Your true essence is this pure, holy soul. Open to the experience of being filled with breath, being breathed. Continue to take deep breaths, relaxing more deeply with each breath.

God breathes into you the levels of soul, *nefesh,* which animates your body. Visualize the letter *hay* from your waist to your legs. God breathes into you the level of soul, *ruach,* which gives you the capacity to feel. Visualize the letter *vav* in your heart. God breathes into you the level of soul, *neshama,* which is the higher self, the capacity to think, to perceive, to know. Visualize the letter *hay* surrounding your head. Be aware that God breathes into you the level of soul *chaya* and *yehida.* These levels of soul surround your body, connect you directly to *Ain Sof.* Visualize the letter *yud* outside your body. With each inhalation, visualize and place each letter in its respective part of your body. See the *hay, vav, hay* and *yud.* Say the letters silently to yourself. On the exhalation, visualize *yud, hay, vav* and the final *hay.* Do this for a few minutes, then be silent, visualize the letters and listen to their sounds within your own breath. God whispers to you His name in your breath. Stay in meditation as long as you like.

4

THE KABBALISTIC TREE OF LIFE

My nine-year-old niece attends a Jewish day school. She has been taught that there is a God and that this God created everything and everyone. She accepts this view without question, but she wonders, "Who created God?" This is a deep question. Everything was created by God, but did God create God? Does God have a Creator? How is this possible? We cannot fathom that God was not created and has no beginning or ending. Everything we know has a beginning and an end. Everything exists within the confines of time and space, yet God is beyond time and space. Kabbalah calls God *Ain Sof* to connect that God is unknowable and limitless, yet, as we learned, *Ain Sof* wanted to be known. This was His original desire, so *Ain Sof* created a God whom we could know and with whom we could interact.

We learned in chapter 3 that when God created the world, He first created the *sephirot*. There are ten *sephirot*. They are the channels through which we experience and know God. Collectively, they are known in kabbalah as the Tree of Life. These *sephirot* appear in all the spiritual worlds, as well as in our world. They are even reflected in our physical bodies. According to kabbalah, when the Bible says that man was created in the image and likeness of God, these words refer to the *sephirot*. When they were first created, the *sephirot* appeared in the shape of a man. The *sephirot* are not separate from the Creator, but they are not the same as the Creator either. They are the channels of light emanating from Him. Always bear in mind that the *sephirot* do not have a separate existence from God. They do not have any life of their own.

The *sephirot* are the ways we experience and know God. They are considered both vessels and lights—vessels because they delineate and limit *Ain Sof* at the same time and lights because they reveal *Ain Sof* in ways that can be received directly. For example, when we say that God is love, we are actually talking about one of the *sephirot*, one of the channels of God's Light. Each *sephirot* has a different name of God associated with it. Together, they constitute the fabric of all the worlds. From the various directions and in various combinations with each other, the *sephirot* shine into this physical world and into us. They merge and interact with each other within us and within this world. The *Zohar* says that a flame needs a wick to burn, so the *sephirot* need the physical world to interact with each other. Though we do not pray to the *sephirot,* we do use them in meditation and in this way we can invoke various divine energies. Different names of God, different letters of the Divine Name and different colors are associated with each *sephirot* and help us access these particular energies in meditation.

The *sephirot,* divided into masculine (right), feminine (left) and central columns, also provide a framework for understanding life and ourselves. As reflections of God, we all have feminine and masculine energies within us. The balance of masculine and feminine energies may vary according to individuals, but each person has both masculine and feminine qualities. The *sephirot* also are associated with different parts of the physical body. In case you are wondering, there is indeed a connection between the seven chakras and the ten *sephirot,* but that is not the subject of this book

As we move in meditative kabbalah, we begin to use the *sephirot* for meditation. We can draw to us these various divine energies. I sometimes suggest to my students that if they want to radiate a certain quality they meditate on the particular Divine Name associated with the *sephira* and wear clothes of the color associated with the *sephira.* This is an ancient kabbalistic practice. For example, to attract the energy of love, wear white. To attract the energy of strength, wear red. We can develop a better balance between the masculine and feminine energies within us by meditating on the various *sephirot* in the body. Some people will find some *sephirot* are easier to experience than others, which indicates the *sephirot* they need to develop.

Meditating and experiencing the *sephirot* in our own bodies is a very powerful, holy and deep spiritual experience. Please do not be discouraged in attempting to do this meditation if you are a beginner to meditation or Judaism. It is an ancient kabbalistic practice, yet it is very New Age because it provides immediate, direct experience of divine energies. Meditating on the *sephirot* is a kind of yoga, providing a unification of the physical body with God. God may be experienced within our own bodies. Job says, "In my own flesh, I experience God." Traditionally, holiness has been understood to mean "to be separate." The soul is holy and separate from the body. The Sabbath is holy because it is separate from the weekdays. God is holy because He is separate from the world. But the experience of holiness we have in meditation is of wholeness. In these moments, the body and the soul are experienced as a single entity. The world and God are united. We experience ourselves not as separate beings but as whole and a part of God. The experience of wholeness is one of profound holiness. The New Age consciousness strives for wholeness and unification. Meditating on the *sephirot* provides a vehicle for awakening such consciousness.

To enjoy the ecstasy of meditative kabbalah, you have to be very familiar with the *sephirot* and able to sense the various energies within your body. Once you are familiar with this information, it will be easier for you to use it in meditation.

Tree of Life Chart

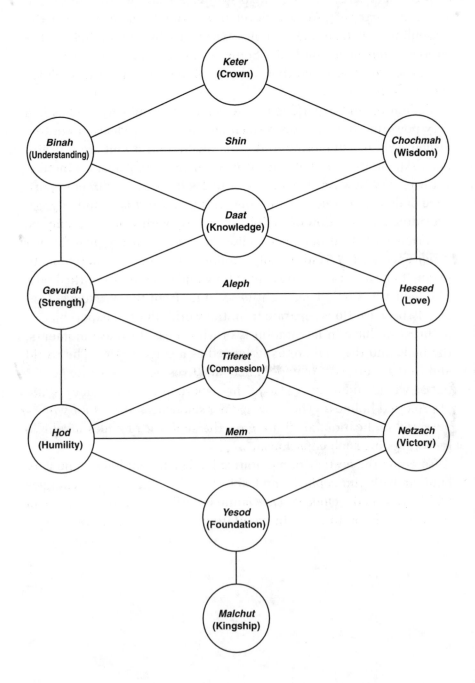

The first *sephira* is *Keter*, the Crown, so called because it is like a crown upon a head, above Creation, above the body. It is the interface between *Ain Sof* and Creation. It is part of *Adam Kadman*, which is the first world God revealed. It is primal existence, prior to the awareness of existence. Because it is closest to *Ain Sof*, it is of the highest quality. On the human psychological level, *Keter* is our internal volition. Everything begins with the will.

The second sephira is known as *Chochmah*. This quality is lower than *Keter*. It is located on the right column. It is the initial flash of wisdom, the beginning of consciousness and recognition. Its inner psychological dimension is selflessness. Emptying the mind allows a new flash to enter.

Binah, the third *sephira,* is the understanding where the flash of *Chochmah* is congealed and comprehended. Its inner psychological dimension is joy. To truly understand is to be joyful.

Chochmah is known as *Abba* (Father) and *Binah* is known as *Ima* (Mother). Judaism is so family oriented, even the *sephirot* are a family constellation. *Chochmah* is the right brain. *Binah* is the left brain. (In some kabbalistic systems, *Binah* is considered the heart.) It is said that *Chochmah* "impregnates" *Binah;* that is, the flash of wisdom enters *Binah,* creating the ability to integrate wisdom in one's being. *Binah* is understanding. It gives form to *Chochmah*. Together, this gives birth to knowledge. *Daat,* knowledge, comes from the union of *Chochmah* and *Binah*. The Torah refers to sexual relations as "knowing." *Daat* is sometimes called a *sephira* and sometimes it is not, depending upon the kabbalistic system. The school of Lubavitch is called Chabad, which is an abbreviation of *Chochmah, Binah* and *Daat*. These *sephirot* are called the *Mohim* in Hebrew, which means "the brains." They are the intellectual *sephirot*.

The next *sephirot,* known as *Zer Anpin,* the "Small Face," referred to as the "Son," are the emotional energies. They bring life, passion and vitality. Since emotions are based on thought, they are the vehicle for the manifestation of thought.

The first *sephira* in *Zer Anpin* is *Hesed,* the attribute of loving-kindness or abundance. The patriarch Abraham is associated with the *sephira* of *Hesed,* as is the right arm. *Hesed* parallels the first day of Creation, the creation of light. Light is a manifestation of *Hesed*. It is the nature of light to illuminate and spread. *Hesed* is the love that has no boundaries, definitions or limitations. It is the energy of boundless giving, as in the desire to give and love boundlessly. "Love makes the world go around," as the song says. Through the energy of *Hesed*, we connect with each other, and we connect with God.

Many people are surprised to find that *Hesed*, appearing on the right column of the kabbalistic paradigm, is considered a masculine attribute. Western culture associates femininity with love and masculinity with being strong, but kabbalah says the opposite: Giving is masculine. Setting boundaries is feminine. When we refer to God as masculine, we call forth the *Hesed* of God, the giving of love and abundance. It is for this reason that God is referred to in the masculine. The name of God, *Elohim*, which was the Divine Name used to create the world, is actually feminine, associated with the energy of *Gevurah*, strength. Creation is actually a concealment, a restriction of Divine Light. Why is giving considered masculine? It was explained to me in *yeshiva* in the following way: In the act of orgasm, the man secretes millions of sperm into the woman who will in turn select only one to be fertilized. At this time, the penis expands, extends and penetrates the vagina, which opens to receive. Bearing in mind the *Hesed* quality of masculinity, the *Zohar* says that the man should pursue the female. The man awakens the desire in the woman by saying loving things to her, sending her flowers, buying her jewelry. Traditionally, the man has been the provider, the giver. He goes out to work to provide for the woman and the family. (In the times of the New Age, the prophet Jeremiah said, this will change—women will court men!)

Hesed (masculine) is limited by the energy of *Gevurah* (feminine). Without *Gevurah*, *Hesed* could not be *Hesed*. To give, we need someone to receive what we have to give. Without a vessel to receive, there can be no giving. Love needs a vessel to contain it, otherwise it is not love. Without a proper vessel to contain *Hesed*, it can actually be destructive. For example, rain is considered an act of *Hesed*. Rain makes nature grow; however, if rain is not contained, not limited, it becomes a flood and brings destruction. Similarly, a teacher restricts himself for a student. If a teacher were to impart to the student everything he knew, the student would be confused. A teacher must restrict what he knows and measure it out according to what the student is able to receive. Love must always be tempered with restraint. It is possible that a person may want to give very much, but unless the giving can be received by a person, it is not an expression of true giving. So true love must be limited and tapered to the recipient; otherwise it overwhelms the receiver. This teaching has important applications to our other human relationships as well.

Gevurah is the ability to contain, to restrict, to set boundaries, to limit and restrain. *Gevurah* is discipline. *Gevurah* is in the left column, associated with the left arm and the color red. It is said that the right hand gives and the left hand pushes away or limits. *Gevurah* expresses strength. *Gevurah* receives from *Hesed* and gives it form and shape. *Gevurah* focuses and channels *Hesed*. *Gevurah* is associated with the patriarch Isaac. Isaac demonstrated *Gevurah* by allowing himself to be sacrificed by his father. The inner psychological dimensions of *Gevurah* are fear and awe. Through restriction, *Gevurah,* we stand back in fear and awe. On a lower level, it may be fear of not being close or of abandonment that causes us to express *Gevurah*.

I find it interesting that *Gevurah* is feminine. If we reflect, we can see that it is often the women who sets boundaries, who bring definition to life. The Jewish woman has always been perceived as strong. Traditionally, she managed the home, raised children, served the community and even ran a business to support the family. In the Bible, it was Sarah who sent her husband's son Ishmael away. It was Rebecca, Isaac's wife, who chose one son over the other to receive the blessing of her husband. In the past, women may have been told that they are the weaker sex, that femininity is a kind of feigned helplessness, but kabbalah reveals that femininity is actually the quality of strength. Women are more discriminating than men. Take a moment to reflect on women you know. Do you see how they manifest *Gevurah* more than men? I have looked at women I know and been amazed to see how women demonstrate *Gevurah* more than men. They may have less power than men, but they are not weaker. Today, women are moving more and more into positions that allow them to publicly use the talents of *Gevurah* they have been given.

The balance, the synthesis between *Hesed* and *Gevurah,* is found in the *sephira* of *Tiferet,* which is beauty, harmony and compassion. *Tiferet* is the central *sephira.* In some kabbalistic systems it is called "truth" or "justice." It is associated with the heart or the solar plexus. Its inner dimension is empathy and mercy, feeling the pain and suffering of another. The desire to heal comes from *Tiferet.* *Tiferet* is accessed through rising above the ego to get a clear picture of what is needed. *Tiferet* is associated with the patriarch Jacob, and its color is yellow or purple.

Hesed, Gevurah and *Tiferet,* the second triad of the *sephirot,* give birth to the third triad: *Netzach,* endurance or victory; *Hod,* splendor or humility; and *Yesod,* foundation or bonding. These *sephirot* bring the knowledge of *Chochmah, Binah* and *Daat* and the emotions of *Hesed, Gevurah* and *Tiferet* into physical form. *Netzach* is associated with the right leg and with Moses. It is persistence, the tenacity to overcome obstacles, commitment. Its inner psychological dimension is trust and self-confidence. This self-confidence must always be rooted in the awareness that God gives you the power to be successful; otherwise, it is negative. The color associated with this *sephira* is light pink. *Netzach* is on the right column, on the masculine side.

Hod, the partner of *Netzach,* is humility. It is also known as splendor or glory. *Hod* allows what is to shine forth and recognizes that all comes from God. The inner psychological dimension is sincerity, doing something for its own sake. *Hod* is associated with the left leg, the feminine column and with Aaron. Together Moses and Aaron led the Jewish people. The color of *Hod* is dark pink.

Yesod is considered the foundation, the vessel that receives all the previous *sephirot* and shapes them into a new form. It is the seat of creativity. It is fulfillment. It is associated with Joseph and the genitals, the seat of Creation. *Yesod* creates a channel between the giver and the receiver, the bonding. It is the seat of holiness. For this reason we must be very careful with our expression of our sexuality. Circumcision occurs in this center. Its inner psychological dimension is truth. What is based on truth will last. It has foundation. The color associated with *Yesod* is orange.

The *sephira* that is considered the ultimate vessel is called *Malchut*. It is a state of being. *Malchut* is kingship, sovereignty and leadership. It is associated with King David. In some kabbalistic systems it is located in the womb, in the mouth, in the speech of a person or outside of the body. This world is called *Malchut* because it receives the spiritual influx from the previous spiritual worlds. *Shabbos* is called *Malchut*. It receives the energy from the previous six days of the week. *Malchut* is feminine. In kabbalah it is known as the daughter.

Meditation on the *Sephirot*

Repeating this meditation several times will make the *sephirot* come alive.

Come to a comfortable seated position for meditation. Close your eyes and take long deep breaths. Breathe through the nostrils and exhale through the mouth, making a sound like a wave in the ocean. . . . Do this several times and continue to take deep inhalations and exhalations through the nostrils. Focus on your breath and follow it inside. With each exhalation, allow yourself to relax more deeply. Now allow the breath to be normal, but continue to focus your attention on it.

Come in contact with your intention and willingness to be a *merkava*, a chariot for the *Shechinah*, the Divine Presence. It is for this you were created. Repeat the following affirmation several times in rhythm with your breath: "I am created in the image and likeness of God." This is the first thing the Torah tells us about man. Your body is a tabernacle for the Divine Presence. The holy emanations meet within your body.

Become aware of the *sephira* of *Keter*, the Crown. It is located above your head. Feel that you are wearing a crown of white light. Now focus your awareness on the head, which is the location of *Chochma*, wisdom. Wisdom emanates from the head. The color of *Chochmah* is said to be a color that includes all other colors. Now open to the *sephira* of *Binah*, understanding, located in your heart. The color is yellow. Breathe into the heart and open to the energy of *Binah*.

Now bring your attention to your right arm and hand, the location of *Hesed*, lovingkindness. The color is white. Open to the *sephira* of *Hesed*. Take deep breaths and breathe in *Hesed*, as to receive God's Hesed.

Now focus your attention on your left arm and hand, which are the seat of *Gevurah*, strength. The color is red. Open to the energy of *Gevurah*. Take a few deep breaths and breathe in *Gevurah*. Ask to be able to radiate *Gevurah* when needed. Alternate your awareness between your right arm and left arm. Appreciate the difference between the *sephirot* of *Hesed* and *Gevurah*.

The balance between *Hesed* and *Gevurah* is reached in the *sephira* of *Tiferet*. *Tiferet* is located in the torso. *Tiferet* is the energy of beauty and compassion. The colors are yellow and purple. It is the middle, the central *sephira*. *Tiferet* is your center. Breathe into the *sephira* of *Tiferet* and let it radiate throughout your entire being.

Now bring your attention to your right leg. This is the seat of *Netzach*, which is endurance, the ability to go through obstacles, victory. The color is light pink. Take deep breaths and open to the energy of *Netzach*, the ability to go through obstacles.

Now bring your attention to your left leg, the seat of *Hod*. *Hod* is humility, splendor, glory. The color is dark pink. Take a few deep breaths and allow the energy of *Hod* to permeate you. Reflect on how the *sephirot* of *Netzach* and *Hod* always go together. *Netzach*, the energy of going forth, must always be balanced by the energy of *Hod*, humility, which allows what is to shine forth.

All these holy energies funnel into the *sephira* of *Yesod*, the foundation or bonding. *Yesod* is located in the genitals. The color is orange. Bring your attention to the pelvic and genital areas, the small, concentrated and vital center of creativity, the center of our sexuality and procreation. Open to the energy of

Yesod. Take a few deep breaths and reflect on the holiness of this center.

The *sephira* of *Yesod* funnels into the *sephira* of *Malchut*, known as the kingdom or sovereignty. *Malchut* is the ultimate vessel for all the *sephirot*. The color is blue. The place of *Malchut* is the mouth or the womb. Visualize your entire body as *Malchut*. The body is the vessel for all the *sephirot*.

Sit in the awareness that all the *sephirot* are within you. They meet within you, and you allow them to interact with each other and be expressed through you. It is only in the physical world that the *sephirot* may interact with each other. The *Zohar* says that a flame needs a wick to burn. The *sephirot* do not interact unless they are connected to the physical. The *sephirot* are within you and are expressed through you. You express love, strength, beauty, compassion, bonding, wisdom, endurance, humility. The *sephirot* interact within you. They are expressed through you.

It is for this you were created. You are created in the image and likeness of God. In your flesh, you shall see God. Experience all the *sephirot* flowing through you.

5

ESTABLISHING A JEWISH
MEDITATION PRACTICE

Meditation and prayer are the most powerful tools now available to us for transforming our consciousness, and Judaism offers a variety of meditation techniques to increase God-awareness. Meditation is an important practice of the New Age as well because it transforms our consciousness in a quick and powerful way. Over the years, I have witnessed the most miraculous transformations of my students through the practice of meditation. Individuals who were highly skeptical, who initially cringed at references to God, have become lovers of God. Those who were "in their head" too much, analytical and critical, have become openhearted and feeling-centered. Meditation is a powerful therapy bringing unification between the soul and the body and emotional integration between the mind and the heart.

However, just meditating is not enough for us to become more loving, compassionate, forgiving and happy people. We must continue to learn about God, to observe God's Will and to work on refining our personal characteristics (middot). Usually these are all intertwined. As we learn more about God and become better people, we are better able to meditate and more willing to surrender our personal will for Divine Will. The traditional Jew is asked to pray and meditate three times each day. Just as we need physical food several times each day, so similarly do we need to nourish ourselves spiritually. Short meditation breaks throughout the day are wonderful.

Through the various teachings and meditations offered in this book, it is my prayer that you will expand your God-awareness and God-connection. The goal of all Jewish practice is to live in the continual awareness of the presence of God. Wherever you go, God is with you. God is within you. Consider for a moment how your life would be transformed if you lived in the awareness of the Divine Presence. I believe you would be happier because you would see the inner dimension of life and experience the beauty, the goodness and wisdom, the unconditional love available in every moment of life.

How do we begin to meditate on a daily or frequent basis? First, learn to breathe correctly; most people do not and, therefore, they cannot relax deeply or focus their concentration properly. Meditation is a state of heightened focus, so we have to learn how to let go of the chatter of the mind and direct our awareness. As you begin a practice in Jewish meditation, it is not necessary that you have any beliefs. The key to your success in meditation is your capacity to be open to yourself, to welcome your meditation experience whatever it may be and to meditate consistently.

This chapter outlines a program for a daily or frequent meditation practice. These meditations are best done in a sitting position but can be quite portable as you move around in the course of a day. These meditations should be safe and beneficial for all people.

FOR BEGINNERS

 ### Conscious Breathing

Correct breathing is diaphragmatic breathing—that is, breathing from the abdomen, to the rib cage, to the chest.

Place one hand on the space between your pelvic bone and

your navel and the other hand high in the chest on your col-larbone. Take long deep breaths, breathing in through the nostrils and exhaling through the mouth, making a sound like a wave in the ocean. Feel free to emit any sound that wants to come out to facilitate the maximum release of tension. Rabbi Nachman recommended that we accentuate a sigh, which releases accumulated tension and stress. Feel free to make any sounds. Do not be inhibited. It feels wonderful to sigh loudly, even to groan. After a few minutes of exhaling through your mouth, emitting any sounds, breathe in and out through the nostrils quietly. Pause comfortably between breaths without strain. Time your breaths. See if you can breathe between two and four breaths per minute. Focus on your breath. Be aware of the gift of life contained within each breath.

 ## Awareness of the Soul

Do a few minutes of conscious deep breathing. Be aware that you do not breathe on your own, but that you are breathed by God. God breathes and sustains you. Allow yourself to let go and open to the love and support contained within each breath. During morning prayers Jews pray with these words: "My God, the soul you placed within me is pure. You created it. You fashioned it. You breathed it into me." God breathes into you a pure soul, which is your true essence. The soul is within the body and also surrounds the body. With each breath, be aware of the levels of the soul: *nefesh, ruach, neshama, chaya* and *yehida.* Experience the descent of the soul into the body, and the ascent of the soul to God. With every breath, feel that you ascend to praise God.

If possible, sit with candlelight. Imagine yourself as a candle. Your body is the candle and the wick, and the soul is the flame. Alternate between gazing at the light of the flame and then seeing yourself as a candle and a flame. Contemplate this: "The soul of man is the candle of God." Pray that you are worthy of truly being a candle of God. This is the true purpose of the soul: to radiate God's Light in the physical world.

Quiet the mind and listen to the needs and desires of the soul within you. Honor the yearnings and feelings of the soul. Feel the soul's desire to expand, to be connected to God. Sit quietly. Let the soul express itself to you and to God. You can do this meditation by yourself, but it would be better if you conclude this meditation with a friend. Ask yourself or your friend "Please tell me what you need and want?" or "How do I nourish my soul?" If you do this meditation with a friend, practice meditative listening—that is, listening fully with your heart and soul. While you are listening, do not think of offering any advice to your partner or about what you are going to say during your sharing. Listen, and look to see and honor the pure soul within your partner.

 ## Speak with God

Talk to God on an ongoing basis. Have a conversation with God about your problems, your desires and your needs. Always ask that you become worthy of coming close to God. Reflect on what you need to do to increase your openness to God. If you like, write to God in your own words. Pick a character trait that causes you problems in your life; usually people choose a variation of anger, depression or low self-esteem. Be aware of how extensive this trait is and how it blocks your capacity to receive God's goodness. Make efforts each day to overcome this trait. Develop a strategy to support this goal. Keep a spiritual accounting of your progress in correcting this trait. Do the *teshuvah* meditations in chapter 9 and seek forgiveness from self, others or God.

 Affirmations

After a few minutes of conscious deep breathing, repeat a short affirmation with the breath each day for five minutes—an "I am _____" statement or a "God is _____" statement. Popular affirmations are "I am lovable and loving," "I accept myself," "God heals me now," "God loves me." If you prefer, take a verse from Psalms and repeat it over and over, such as "God is my Light and salvation." If you can do this meditation with a friend, you will each experience a great treat. Each of you should say your affirmation to the other. Your partner will then repeat your affirmation to you. To do this, you say, "You, [state your partner's name], [state the affirmation]." For example, "You, Steve, love and accept yourself." Do this several times. Then change to the third-person voice: "He, Steve, loves and accepts himself." Do this several times. If you can do this with a larger group, it will be even more powerful.

 Be in the Center of God

Each day center yourself in the awareness of being in the center of God. God is the center within you, and you are within God. Repeat this to yourself: "I am in the center of God." Take a few deep breaths and open yourself to experience this truth. Let your consciousness expand in all six directions. Imagine that you can transcend the physical world of limitations and touch infinity. Feel the tremendous sense of freedom and love available when you allow yourself to expand. God is within you, and you are within God. Pause for a few moments and take several long, deep breaths.

Do this meditation any time. It is wonderful to practice this meditation while you are walking, even during errands.

Pray

Pray each day with the traditional Jewish prayer book. It is not necessary for you to say all the prayers three times a day; however, it is recommended that you do the preliminary blessings, a psalm or two, the *Shema,* and the Standing *Amidah* prayer at least once a day. Take time to savor the words of the prayers, particularly the *Amidah* prayer, where you place yourself in the presence of God. Say some of the prayers very slowly, pausing to deepen your breath. Pray for the needs and the healing of yourself and others.

 Offer Blessings

Offering blessings is the most powerful and direct way to connect with the source of all blessings. Blessing yourself and others increases blessings in your own life. Following are some suggestions for increasing blessings in your life:

- Offer blessings before and after eating food. Say each word of the blessing slowly. Take a breath between each word of the blessing so as to contemplate and absorb its personal meaning and teaching to you in this moment. Eat slowly and consciously. Become a vegetarian or eat kosher.
- Light *Shabbos* candles on Friday night. Say each word of the candle blessing slowly. Visualize yourself surrounded by God's Light and peace. Send this light to loved ones. See them surrounded by it. Begin to keep the Sabbath, if you are not doing so already. Take on other *mitzvot* like saying *Kiddush,* wearing a *tallis,* putting on *tefillin,* etc. Consult with a rabbi if you want some guidance.
- Place yourself in a meditative state by deep breathing. Imagine that the top of your head opens and you experience yourself as a vessel, open and ready to receive. Feel

that you can breathe through the top of your head. Feel your desire to receive God's Light and love and blessing. Sing a *niggun,* if you like. Repeat to yourself "*Yehi Or,*" which means "Let there be light." These were the first words of God recorded in the Torah. Say them silently and then out loud. "Let me be worthy to experience God's holy light." Imagine that you can draw down white healing, loving light. This light enters the top of your head and flows through your entire body. Breathe and bask in the light.

- Place yourself in a meditative state. Imagine that the light of the *Shechinah* is above your head, entering and surrounding you. Raise your hands up to the heavens and feel the energy in them. Open to being a channel for divine blessings. Envision the image of a person you would like to bless. Utter a blessing in your mind. You might want to begin with these words: "May you be blessed _____." "May God bless you _____." "You are blessed with _____." Continue to allow the outpouring in your heart and soul to be expressed. Visualize the person surrounded by the light of the Divine Presence.

 ## Experience Godliness

The whole world is filled with Godliness. Everything happens to teach you something, to deepen you and bring you closer to God. What is your spiritual opportunity today? Practice receiving everything in your life with grace and gratitude. If you like, take time for writing in your journal. Write the following words in your journal and write from a stream of consciousness: "Now is a time in my life when I _____" or "Today was a day when I _____."

FOR THE INTERMEDIATE MEDITATOR

These meditations are for individuals who are sincerely dedicated to their spiritual growth, who are committed to Jewish practice and have been meditating consistently for at least a year. Individuals with a psychiatric problem or emotional illness are advised to refrain from these meditations. It is also essential that you be totally familiar with the concepts outlined in chapter 3 and the *sephirot* outlined in chapter 4. If you become dizzy or nauseous doing these meditations, please stop and concentrate for a minimum of six months on the beginner meditations.

Meditating on the Divine Names is powerful because we summon the divine emanations. In Psalms 91:14 it is written, "I will raise him up because he knows my name." Contemplating and repeating the name brings knowledge and intimacy with God. In an ancient kabbalistic book, *Shaari Orah: Gates of Light,* it is written, "Each of the Holy Names has a unique function. . . . One should be aware that all the names mentioned in the Torah are the keys for anything a person needs in the world. There are Names in charge of prayer, mercy and forgiveness, while others are in charge of tears and sadness, injury and tribulations, sustenance and income, heroism, loving-kindness and grace. If one does not know how to concentrate on the very Name which is the key to the answer of his request, then who is to blame if the request is not granted. . . . It is the foolishness of man that is to blame. . . . God is open to everyone."

✡ Intermediate Meditation 1: On the Divine Name

Place yourself in a meditative state. See the letters of the Divine Name in front of you. Carve out each letter individually. See the *Yud*, the *Hay*, the *Vav* and the final *Hay*. Now breathe the *Yud* into your head, exhale the *Hay* into your shoulders and arms, breathe the *Vav* into your torso, and exhale the *Hay* into your waist and legs. Alternate between seeing the letters on your outer screen and seeing them within your body. Then say the Divine Name *Adonoy* silently to yourself as you visualize it in your body and on your inner screen. According to the Arizel, the name *Adonoy* is a treasure chest of blessings. Keep repeating the name as you visualize the letters.

✡ Intermediate Meditation 2: On the Permutations of the Divine Name

Place yourself in a meditative state. Say the permutations of the letters of the Divine Name silently to yourself. Do not say them out loud. Breathe *Yah* into your head, seeing the letter *Yud* for the count of ten. Exhale *Hah* to the count of five, seeing the letter *Hay* in your heart. Breathe in light with the *Yud* and radiate this light through the heart with the *Hay*. Do this for several minutes. The more love you can radiate, the more light you will receive. Let God's Light and love flow through you.

If you like, deepen the meditation by continuing the above meditation. Breathe in *Yah,* seeing the letter *Yud* in your head. Exhale *Hah,* seeing the letter *Hay* in your heart. Breathe in *Vah,* seeing the letter *Vav* in your torso and exhaling the final *Hah,* seeing the letter *Hay* in your waist and legs. Do this several times. Now repeat this meditation in the same way, doing the permutation of all the vowel sounds. Breathe in *Yeh*. Exhale *Heh*. Breathe in *Veh*. Exhale *Heh*. Do this several times. Then breathe in *Yay*. Exhale *Hay*. Inhale *Vay*. Exhale *Hay*. Do this several times. Breathe in *Yi*. Exhale *Hi*. Inhale *Vi*. Exhale *Hi*. Do this several times. Then breathe in *Yoh*. Exhale *Hoh*. Inhale *Voh*. Exhale *Hoh*. Do this several times. Then breathe in *Yoo*. Exhale *Hoo*. Inhale *Voo*. Exhale *Hoo*. Do this several times. Let the letters radiate inside you.

✡ Intermediate Meditation 3: On the *Sephirot* and Vowel Permutations

While in a meditative state, visualize the name of God: *yud, hay, vav, hay*. Place the Divine Name with the various vowel permutations as they relate to the various *sephirot*. During this meditation, you will say the various permutations of the Divine Name *silently* to yourself. The Arizel issued a warning about saying the names out loud.

Begin by visualizing the Divine Name on the top of your head, as if you are wearing a crown. Open to the energy of *Keter*. See the Divine Name with the *kametz* vowel: *Yah, Hah, Vah, Hah*. Then see the Divine Name float into your head.

Open to the energy of *Chochmah* and visualize *Yah, Hah, Vah, Hah* (see the letters with the vowel *patach*). Let the letters radiate in your head in white light with a black background or black letters amid a white-light background. Float the letters down your neck to your heart. Open to the energy of *Binah*. See the letters of the Divine Name with the *tzere: Yay, Hay, Vay, Hay*. Let your heart be filled with yellow light.

Now bring the Divine Name to your right arm, the seat of *Hesed*. The permutation *(segol)* is *Yeh, Heh, Veh, Heh*. Open to the energy of *Hesed*. Let your arm be filled with white light. Now bring the Divine Name to your left arm, the seat of *Gevurah*. The vowel is the *sheva* (silent): *Y. H. V. H.* The color is red. Now bring the Divine Name to your torso, to the seat of *Tiferet*. The vowel permutation is *cholem: Yoh, Hoh, Voh, Hoh*. The color is purple. Open to the energy of *Tiferet*.

Now bring the Divine Name to your right leg, to the seat of *Netzach*. The vowel permutation is *chirek: Yi, Hi, Vi, Hi*. The color is light pink. Now bring the Divine Name to your left leg, the seat of *Hod*. The vowel is *kibbutz: Yu, Hu, Vu, Hu*. The color is light pink. Open to the energy of *Hod*. Now bring the Divine Name to your genital area. The vowel permutation is the *shurek: Yu, Hu, Vu, Hu*. The color is orange.

This is the foundation. Now feel your entire body as a vessel. This is the *sephira* of *Malchut*. Some say it is located in the womb or the mouth, but for this meditation, see the entire body as a vessel. *Malchut* is the ultimate vessel. Place the *Yud* in your head, the *Hay* in your heart, the *Vav* in your solar plexus, the final *Hay* in your waist and legs. There are no vowels for this *sephira*.

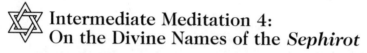

Intermediate Meditation 4: On the Divine Names of the *Sephirot*

Place yourself in a meditative state. Ask that you be worthy to be a chariot for the Divine Presence. Bring your awareness to the top of your head, the seat of *Keter,* and repeat the Divine Name *Ehyeh Asher Ehyeh* silently to yourself for several minutes. Immerse yourself in a brilliant white light. Now bring your awareness to the head, the seat of *Chochmah,* and repeat the name *Yah* silently to yourself. The color of *Chochmah* is the color of fire, or a color that includes all colors. Now bring your awareness to the heart, the seat of *Binah.* Visualize the *YHVH* and say *"Elohim"* silently for a few minutes. The color is yellow. Now bring your attention to your right arm, the seat of *Hesed.* The Divine Name is *El.* The color is white. Say this name silently to yourself for a few minutes as you open to the energy of *Hesed.* Then bring your attention to your left arm, the seat of *Gevurah.* The Divine Name associated with this *sephira* is *Elohim.* The color is red. Say this name as you open to the energy of *Gevurah.* Now bring your attention to your torso, the seat of *Tiferet.* The Divine Name is *YHVH,* pronounced as *A-do-noy.* The color is purple. See the name and say *"Adonoy"* silently for a few minutes. Then bring your focus to your right leg, the seat of *Netzach.* The Divine Name is *Adonoy Tzevaot.* The color is light pink. See the name and say it silently for a few minutes as you open to the energy of *Netzach.* Then bring your awareness to your left leg, the seat of *Hod.* The Divine Name is *Elohim Tzevaot.* The color is dark pink. Say this name silently to yourself for a few minutes as you open to the energy of *Hod.*

Then bring your awareness to your genital area, the seat of *Yesod*. The Divine Name is *Shaddai* or *El Chai*. The color is orange. Say this name silently, opening to the energy of *Yesod*. Then bring your attention to your mouth, the seat of *Malchut*. The Divine Name is *Adonoy*. The color is blue. Say this name silently for a few minutes. This Divine Name is the closest to us. It is considered the primary gate.

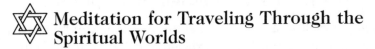

Meditation for Traveling Through the Spiritual Worlds

Take a few deep breaths to center yourself. Begin by becoming aware of the physical world and imagine that the whole world is enclosed in the letter *hay*. Now visualize the letter *hay* around your body. You sit in the letter *hay*. This is the world of *Assiyah*. Breathe and enjoy the protection of the letter *hay*. Now become aware that there is an angelic world. This is the world of *Yetzirah*. We are surrounded by angels. Visualize the letter *vav* a few inches above the top of your head and imagine that there are angels traveling up and down the letter *vav*. Imagine that the *vav* is a conductor of blessing and Divine Light. Now see the light of the *vav* entering into the letter *hay*, which is directly above it. The letter *hay* is filled with Divine Light. This is the world of *Beriyah*. Above the letter *hay*, visualize the letter *yud*, a small point from which all the worlds emanate. All Creation began with a point. All the energy of Creation is concentrated in this point. This is the world of *Atzilut*. This is the point of unity. Travel upward through the spiritual worlds a few times with your breath. Visualize the letters in their various positions as you reflect on each spiritual world.

Now do this meditation in reverse order. Visualize the *yud*, that concentrated point, twelve inches above the top of your head. Under the *yud* visualize the *hay* and imagine that the light spreads through the *hay*. The *yud* and the *hay* are the

Divine Light coming from the highest worlds. Under the *hay* visualize the *vav*. The *vav* is the straight line that channels the light to our world. Now see the light pour into the letter *hay*, which surrounds your body. Repeat this visualization a few times.

With each inhalation, breathe from the world of *Assiyah* and visualize the letter *hay*. Then breathe from the world of *Yetzirah* and visualize the letter *vav*. Next, breathe from the world of *Beriyah* and visualize the letter *hay*. Now breathe from the world of *Atzilut* and see the letter *yud*. On the exhalation, see the *yud* spread into the letter *hay* and then the letter *vav* and then the letter *hay*. On each breath, ascend through the spiritual worlds, and on each exhalation descend.

PART TWO

JEWISH SELF-HELP

6

ACCESSING THE DIVINE BLUEPRINT

Many of us do not have personal mission statements for our lives. All too often we react to people and events rather than creating what we want in our lives. We run around meeting our physical and emotional needs, as well as those of others, and have little time left for much else. Rabbi Nachman asked us to reflect each day whether we are living lives worthy of the pure souls we have been given. We have to consider whether we are living the lives that we want. Our lives have meaning and purpose when we live with intention and vision. If we know and understand God's original purpose for creating the world and align our personal intention with God's, we will find ourselves more fully engaged in the flow of our lives that God envisioned and able to receive all the goodness He intended.

The kabbalistic paradigm for creation of the four worlds (as presented in chapter 3) is a powerful framework for creating what we want in our lives. Though God creates something from nothing and we always create something from something, we must go through a similar process of mirroring the divine when we are actively creative in our lives. To bring forth our vision, to create something new in our lives, we need to empty, we need to contract, to do a *tzimtzum* to allow something new to come forth. As God did a *tzimtzum,* so do we. To develop a new vision of what we ultimately want to bring forth in our lives, we need to take time to quiet ourselves and withdraw from the constant activity with which we busy ourselves.

It is important that we give ourselves the time and respect to reflect on what the purpose of our life is. To do this, we need the will and desire to create. This happens at the level of the first world, *Atzilut.* Then we must consider a plan and the strategies by which we will actualize our vision. This is like an architect's plan. This is the level of the second world, *Beriyah.* Next, we need to know and put in place all that we need to accomplish our goal. What are the resources, the tools needed? This is the level of the third world, *Yetzirah.* To implement and carry out the plan, we access the fourth world, *Assiyah.*

According to New Age thought, we shape our own lives by our thoughts, our speech and our deeds. We are not victims, nor are we powerless. This perspective emphasizes a person's creative abilities and personal responsibility. According to kabbalah, it is no accident that the head is above the heart. Everything begins with intention. In Judaism the heart is the center, providing the passion, but the head should direct the heart.

Take a few moments now to contemplate your mission statement for your life and let the following questions for deep self-inquiry— questions to be reflected upon through life—guide you:

Why are you here on Earth?
What is really important to you?
What do you want to accomplish in your life?
If someone were to talk about your life, what would be said about you? How would you like to be remembered?

Take a few moments to write your responses in your journal. It is okay not to know the answers to these questions, and it is good to speak or write about the not-knowing because life is about self-discovery.

Record whether or not the activities of your life are supporting your mission statement. How much time each day or each week do you devote to accomplishing your goals? If you have a good friend who is also reading this book, take time to ask each other these questions and provide a listening presence for each other.

Mission statements and how closely they correspond to our life purpose vary widely from person to person. For example, I might have a mission statement that I want to learn Torah, that I want to help other people or that I want to be physically fit. Though I might have identified this as a primary life purpose, when I look at how I live my life, I might find that I actually devote very little time to what is important to me. To evaluate whether or not the activities of your life are supporting your mission statement, ask yourself another key question: How much time each day or each week do you really devote to accomplishing your goals?

APPLYING THE DIVINE BLUEPRINT TO YOUR LIFE

The Level of *Atzilut*

State your vision of how you would like to see yourself in the next year. What are your desires and goals? Why? Be very clear about your purpose. Make a visionary affirmation about your life.

Example: "I see myself physically fit. Being physically fit, I have more energy to enjoy my life and do what I need to do."

The Level of *Beriyah*

What is your overall plan?
Example: "To be physically fit, I need a plan of diet, exercise and recreation. I will gather all the information I need to determine what is a reasonable goal for me."

The Level of *Yetzirah*

What are the tools and activities you need to actualize your goal?
Example: "I will alter my diet and begin to exercise. I will eliminate snacking between meals, eating desserts and sugar. I will exercise thirty minutes per day."

The Level of *Assiyah*

Implement your vision and verify that you are doing what you intended.

Example: "I will implement my vision. Am I doing what I intended?"

THE DIVINE BLUEPRINT IN INTIMACY AND PARTNERSHIPS

This kabbalistic model may also be used to understand ourselves and what is happening in our relationships with others and with our communities. The deepest and most satisfying relationships we have with people extend through all the worlds.

At the level of *Atzilut*, we share a common vision and desire. We cannot have real intimacy and commitment with another person unless we have a common vision that recognizes and appreciates that the partnership is needed to actualize this vision. It is this common vision that provides the foundation and glue for the partnership. At the level of *Beriyah*, we agree on the overall plan for implementing our vision. At the level of *Yetzirah*, we identify capabilities and responsibilities. At the level of *Assiyah*, we implement and live the plan and vision.

Following is a brief summary of this blueprint:

Atzilut: What is the vision and intention for the partnership?
Briyah: How will we implement this vision?
Yetzirah: Who will do what?
Assiyah: Is the vision viable? Does it flow easily? (If not, identify the problem.)

THE DIVINE BLUEPRINT
FOR PERSONAL HEALING

One of the greatest obstacles people have in bringing forth what they want in their lives is the feeling of unworthiness. Because of negative messages people have received in childhood and through painful life experiences, they feel defeated and hopeless. They are not able to access the wonderful creative energies within them. They consciously or unconsciously give messages to themselves such as "I am not enough," "I don't deserve better than I have" or "I am no good." (Do any of these sound familiar to you?) It's no wonder people feel bad repeating these thoughts over and over. Such negative messages need to be replaced with positive ones. For this, the practice of affirmations is vital. It will uplift and transform you. It is important to keep in mind that affirmations are simple, succinct, positive statements in the present tense that are true statements about God or about the Divine Soul that is your true essence.

Using affirmations is a popular New Age practice, but it is also an ancient kabbalistic one. For example, kabbalists like to take a phrase of Psalms and repeat it over and over. To try this approach, do the following meditation:

 ## Meditation for Personal Healing

Atzilut: Articulate an "I am" statement or a "God is" statement.

Take a few deep breaths so you are in a somewhat altered state. Then make your "I am" or "God is" statement from the level of *Atzilut,* such as "I am loving and lovable" or "I am a creature of God" or "I am a radiant channel of God's Light and love." Using your affirmation, breathe it in upon inhalation and say it again upon exhalation. Do this several times. Repeat the affirmation only on the inhalation and allow the affirmation to enter deeply within you upon exhalation. Do this meditation for a few minutes several times each day.

These affirmation statements are on the level of identity. This is who you really are. This is the person God created you to be. Agree to reflect this higher vision of yourself. It is also very powerful to make a "God is" statement, such as "God is good" or "God is love" or "God is merciful" or "God is forgiving." Make it more personal with affirmations such as "God loves me" or "God gives me strength." Repeat this statement in the same fashion as the previous affirmations.

Beriyah: How would it feel to live this affirmation? Imagine what your life would look like if you were living this affirmation? See yourself expressing the affirmation. Imagine that as a child you knew this about yourself. See yourself as a child, radiating this affirmation.

Yetzirah: What do you need to do to begin to actualize the affirmation—that is, to ground it into your being, your body, your soul and practically manifest it in your world? What kinds of support do you need?

Assiyah: Live your affirmation. Continue to repeat it. Be aware when your mind returns to negative thinking patterns. Exhale these thoughts through your breath and return to your affirmation.

7

BECOMING A SERVANT OF GOD

I have always been deeply moved by the words of the prophet Hosea, who lets us know that in the future our principal mode of relationship with God will be as a lover and not as a servant. This prophecy predicts the spiritual paradigm of the New Age, a time when we will enjoy the experience of unity with God. Through the prophet Hosea, God says, "You will call me My Husband, and you will no longer call me My Master. . . . I shall marry you to Me forever. I shall marry you to Me with righteousness, and with justice, and with kindness, and with mercy. I shall marry you to Me with fidelity, and you shall know God" (Hos. 2:18).

These are the actual words a Jew says each day when putting *tefillin*—leather prayer scrolls—on the head and left arm. Marriage with the divine is a metaphor for the ultimate spiritual experience and greatest joy. It is the greatest gift God gives us. At times, a mystically oriented person dedicated to the love and service of God is rewarded and blessed with a taste of this more intense kind of intimacy with the divine.

Until then, being a servant of God is the mainstream Jewish mode of relationship with the divine. In this way, we open to a spiritual life and deepen the connection with God. Experiencing ourselves as

71

God's servant is actually a great privilege and an opportunity to actualize our deepest inner potential. By dedicating ourselves to attributes greater than ourselves, we become greater. If we dedicate
ourselves to God, who is loving and compassionate, who is
absolutely free, who is eternal, we will absorb, experience and radiate these qualities as well. When we move closer to God, God moves
close to us. In the process of serving God, the ego mind is restrained,
the limited sense of self is diminished and the soul becomes more
prominent. We experience ourselves as greater than we thought we
were.

Though there are many spiritual gifts from spiritual service, such
service is misunderstood and resented by many people today. Today
we all want to experience ourselves as free people, not as servants.
Considering ourselves as servants goes against the western ethos of
independence and democracy. We want to be the ones making
things happen in our lives and in the lives of other people. We want
to be doers and shakers. We do not want to be subservient because
that means we are not in control—and being in control is very
important to us. Furthermore, we do not want to be controlled or
manipulated by fear and guilt, which is often the language employed
by traditional religion.

I can appreciate that many men and women are uncomfortable
hearing God called "King." What occurs within you when you contemplate the idea of God as King of the World. How does it expand
or contract your consciousness to hear these words? What does it
mean to you? What does it say about the world?

Personally, I find the metaphor of God as King to be powerful and
transformational. I love Rosh Hashanah, when many of our prayers
acknowledge God as King. It implies to me that there is a divine
order to the world. When I say that God is King, or I want God to be
King, I am really saying that I want a world where everyone is
devoted to fostering the consciousness of unity so that the oneness
of God, the underlying true reality that unifies all existence, pervades the world. When I aspire to reach God as King, I experience
myself as a servant of this high goal. If God is acknowledged as King,
it is easy and safe for me to relinquish my personal ego and sense of
separateness to the higher truth. Envisioning God as King restores

my deepest hope and desire to see the fulfillment of God's original vision of creating the world to bestow goodness, founded on truth and justice realized. Rabbi Yitzchok Luria, the Arizel, said that when we say that God is King, we recognize that God is giving us existence at this very moment. Everything is constantly being recreated anew. This is an awesome and liberating awareness.

The traditional metaphor of God as King may not be so effective for New Age practitioners. Kings in our day do not have the power they once did. They are merely ceremonial figureheads. In all likelihood, I suspect that God was called "King" in the prayer book because the world was dominated by kings and queens when the sages who composed the liturgy lived. Every country had a king or a queen who had considerable power over the daily lives of subjects, so it was easy for people to transfer to God the fear and loyalty they felt toward an earthly monarch. (It has occurred to me that Judaism may have introduced democracy to the world by calling God "King" and limiting the powers of human kings and queens.)

The king of Israel was not considered to be a god as kings in many countries were. When Israel was a monarchy, the king was subject to certain restrictions to limit abuse of power. He could not assemble too much military power, lest he think he did not need God for protection. He had to scribe a Torah and read certain sections daily to remind him of the Almighty and of his own unique position of service. He was not considered an intermediary to God on behalf of the people. He shared power with the priestly branches of the nation, the Levites and the Cohanim, who performed religious functions in the Holy Temple. He also had to answer to the prophets, who were seen as divinely inspired by God.

The model of king and servant is said by some to be associated with the old spiritual paradigm. It is not considered a New Age concept. I suspect that much of the current resistance to calling God "King" goes deeper than the male or political inferences. People are alienated by the distance implied in a relationship between a king and a servant. It feels undemocratic, authoritarian. Today, people want a more intimate connection with God, to be partners with Him. We seek union with God. We want to love God, not fear Him. We want to experience God within ourselves. We want God on our own terms.

Many are uncomfortable with the idea of surrendering their personal will, even to a higher, more perfected will, as implied in a relationship between king and servant. Some are frightened by the
concept. Many of us may have experienced exploitation, manipula-
tion or abuse by others. Some parents used the idea of God to control or punish their children. Having grown up as victims of a
consumer society, where everything is packaged and sold through
seductive advertising, we are terribly afraid of being exploited and
humiliated by religion. In the modern world, most everything is
related to business. The marketplace mentality pervades all aspects
of our life and inner being. Life seems like a large shopping center
and people are very consumer driven. The values of society instruct
people to watch out for themselves. It is hard to know who to trust
or whether we can trust at all.

As a society, we are self-oriented, self-interested and self-
absorbed. Even our spirituality is marketed, as witnessed in the
vibrant spiritual marketplace of the New Age. Various spiritual dis-
ciplines and techniques compete for practitioners, each one making
more and more amazing promises and claims. We cannot be so naive
as to think that all these techniques will deliver the happiness they
promise. In actuality, some may guide us down a path that leads to
greater self-indulgence, alienation and, ultimately, despair.

According to Judaism, the true happiness and enlightenment
people seek, often desperately, in their lives comes more from giving
than from receiving. Paradoxically, a person looking for happiness
has to relinquish or nullify the self to find what the self really wants.
This is achieved best by giving, for in true acts of giving, we transcend ego and overcome self-absorption. We then discover that our
center is not within ourselves as we originally thought. We find that
our true center lies in God, the ultimate giver. By giving, the walls
separating us from God are diminished and we no longer feel isolated but experience ourselves as a part of God, a channel for God's
love. Rabbi Eliyahu Dessler, a leading rabbi in the Mussar movement
of the nineteenth century, said that a person cannot truly believe in
God unless he is a giving person.

Giving is a powerful spiritual practice through which we become
like God. In kabbalah, closeness is not marked by physical proximity

but by resemblance. For example, people can be physically close, but if they are very different in their qualities, they are not close in the spiritual sense. Spiritually, we are close to what we resemble. Since God is the ultimate giver, we become close to God by becoming givers. If we give to bring more love and unity into this world, without ulterior motive or expectation of return, we are truly open to God. And then God gives to us in the sweetest and most abundant ways.

In the words of Rabbi Gamliel recorded in *Ethics of the Fathers,* "Treat God's Will as if it were your own will and He will treat your will as if it were His Will. Nullify your will before His Will and He will nullify the will of others before your will." God protects His servants. God's servants are people who experience and radiate a deep sense of peace and well-being regardless of what the external circumstances of their lives are and people often sense this. Even when they are suffering, they experience that God is always with them. Such people trust that good will come from everything. They believe that ultimately everything comes from God, and therefore that everything that happens has meaning and purpose. This kind of connection to God brings personal freedom, meaning and depth not otherwise possible.

God promises us, "Be my servants and you will not be servants to anyone else" *(Ethics of the Fathers).* A person who is a true servant of God is actually freer and more courageous than the average person. There is a well-known story of a previous Lubavitcher rebbe who was arrested during the pre-Stalin Era. A gun was put to his head and he was asked to make a confession for something he did not do. The Russian officer, while holding a gun, said to him, "This toy makes people change their minds." The rebbe responded, "It will do that for people who believe in one world and many gods, but I believe in one God and many worlds, and I am not afraid." He was released.

Being a servant of God means doing what is right, doing what is proper even though it may not be immediately gratifying. This role brings strength and meaning to us. It builds character and a sense of personal integrity. This is true freedom. A servant of God is not the victim of other people or circumstances. The prophet Jeremiah tells us that a person who places his trust in people and not in God will be "like a lone tree in the wilderness and not see when goodness comes" (Jer. 17:6). If we place our trust in people, we will be disappointed. We have to learn to place our trust in God and not in people. As good-hearted as we may be, we are limited.

As servants of God, we do not have to compromise what we think is right or important for a temporary need. Though we are loving to all people, we do not have to debase ourselves or be a people-pleaser to get what we want. We can be trusted and respected by others. We know that everything comes from God. "Blessed is the man who trusts in God. God will be his security. He will be like a tree that is planted near water, which will spread its roots alongside brooks and not see when heat comes, whose foliage will be always fresh, who will not worry in years of drought and never stop producing fruit" (Jer. 17:7). As servants of God, we feel that God loves us and is taking care of us at all times.

In one of the many stories recorded in the Mishnah, part of the Oral Torah, a Jew purchases a field from a non-Jew. After some time, he discovers that there is a treasure buried in the field. He returns the treasure to the original owner who obviously had not known that a treasure was buried on his property. The non-Jew rejoiced, proclaiming, "What a great God you must have that you returned the treasure to me." By this act of service, the Jew honored God. Because this story was recorded, it remains available for us to read and emulate.

In his profound book *The Longer Shorter Way*, Rabbi Adin Steinhaltz asks a question that we should be particularly mindful of and meditate upon: "Do I want the feeling that I am close to God or do I want the actual experience of being close to God?" This is a deep and challenging question. Doing what God wants may not always bring the immediate gratification of a spiritual high. Some people feel themselves spiritually expanded and enjoy a sense of intoxication from spiritual practices, but it is their egos that become larger as a result, and their professed spirituality has not been integrated into their being. When people do not become more loving, more conscious, better human beings as a result of their involvement in spirituality or religion, we may question whether they are having a true spiritual or truly religious experience. Might they be deceiving themselves?

To become a true servant of God, we must wage an internal battle between the inner soul, which wants to nullify itself before God, and the ego, which wants to be in control, to receive, to be recognized and honored. Being a servant of God is not such an easy position to achieve and maintain. It is a lifelong process and can sometimes be achieved only in degrees. Many people want to be connected to something greater than themselves, but if they look into their hearts and souls, they find that even their service to God is overlaid by their self-interest and ego needs. They may want God—but only on their own terms. This is one criticism that traditionalists have with New Age people, but wanting God on our own terms is also very common among people who are religiously devout and traditionally committed.

Bachya Ibn Paquda, a twelfth-century mystic, wrote a dialogue between two aspects of himself, the soul and the mind, in his book *Duties of the Heart*. He explored some of the resistance and challenge we face in being servants of God. He said that, in most cases, people express thankfulness to God and even take a step in serving Him, but they do this not really to serve God for God's sake but for what they are going to gain from their service. If we examine the true motivation underlying our actions, whether they be in the spiritual, emotional or work arena of our lives, we will most likely find that much of what we do is calculated. We do things because we want physical pleasures, comfort, recognition, honor, remuneration. We're always thinking about what we can gain from others and even what we can gain from God. This is part of our human nature. The desire to receive is embedded within us because God wants to give to us.

Even in the spiritual arena we are encouraged to perform a spiritual action in order to receive a certain material benefit. For example, we are told to say certain prayers for healing, marriage or children. This is acceptable: We are taught in the Talmud that we have needs because God wants us to call upon Him. It is fine to say a prayer or do a *mitzvah*, which is an action prescribed by Jewish law, because we want to receive something from God. It is a means of having a relationship with God. However, we may pray for something seemingly without success, and if we undertake a spiritual action solely because we want a reward, we may have a crisis of faith when we do not get the immediate gratification we seek for our spiritual efforts. Our prayers are not always answered in the way or with the speed that we want. This may be frustrating or painful. However, rather than discontinuing our prayers, we may consider changing our prayers to ask for the strength and the patience to accept and learn from our current situation and do whatever opening and preparation we can to receive the blessings we are requesting.

Central to our spiritual practice is the recognition that God is the source of all life and all blessings and that it is God who will bring forth what we want. This awareness will transform and elevate us. Over time, through continual prayer and spiritual practice, what we want will become more refined. We will come to find that the greatest good we can receive from God is the experience of closeness with Him. Nothing can compare to this. Soon this will be all we ask for.

Many people want to understand what they do and what they will receive from their actions. They want to do things that make them feel good. Of course it is best that we do our religious or spiritual practice with feeling, understanding and pleasure rather than by rote or out of obligation. However, if we can do something just because we are commanded to do so, and simply because we want to make the connection with God, we will experience more joy from the practice than if we did the practice because it made sense to us or because we expected to benefit materially or socially from it. It is actually a very liberating experience to do something that is not motivated by personal gain. If you do not know personally what this means, experience the pleasure of giving—not because you expect to receive something in return—and witness what occurs within you.

Service to God for the Jewish people began when they accepted the Torah at Mount Sinai. They said in one voice, "We will do, and then we will understand." By saying these words, the Jewish people affirmed that they were willing to fulfill God's Will even if at first they did not understand. This is the highest level of service and devotion. The Torah gives very clear instructions, a blueprint, for serving God in all aspects of our lives. Torah is not just the Ten

Commandments or the Five Books of Moses. Torah includes kabbalah, Torah commentary, Jewish law and everything written that elucidates everything that came before. The elaborate and pervasive system of prescribed commandments known as *mitzvot,* the do's and the don'ts of Judaism, provide designated avenues for strengthening our personal connection with God.

The Hebrew word *mitzvah,* which is the singular form of *mitzvot,* means "to connect." *Mitzvot* are generally physical acts that make connections between a person and God, as well as between people. The *mitzvot* bring about healing and a sense of wholeness because they involve the body, the mind, the heart and the soul in one simple act that has been commanded by God. Most *mitzvot* require us to perform a simple action and say a blessing before or after it. *Mitzvot* have the ability to give us a taste of transcendence and holiness while allowing this holiness to be integrated into daily life. People who do *mitzvot* with the proper consciousness are better grounded in the mundane and physical dimensions of life. Some *mitzvot* create community because they require a certain number of people to accomplish them; for example, certain prayers can only be said in the presence of ten people.

According to kabbalists, *mitzvot* do more than unite the person who is performing them; they also redeem God and the world. Though God's oneness is not revealed in this world, godly sparks are hidden within everything in the physical world, and when we take something physical, something mundane, and bring God-consciousness to the act, we release the holy, hidden God sparks within the physical act and thereby bring God into this world. Before prayer and the performance of a *mitzvot,* a kabbalistic intention is recited to unify the God who is transcendent with the *Shechinah,* the immanence of God. This unification is much like what we do when we say the *Shema.* All *mitzvot* actually bring unification to the name of God. Religious Jews believe that they are bringing in the New Age by their simple actions of *mitzvot.*

Mitzvot pervade every aspect of life, from getting up in the morning, going to the bathroom, eating and working, to sleeping. These physical and potentially mundane aspects of life are sanctified and elevated through the practice of the *mitzvot* related to them. There are all kinds of *mitzvot* for a total of 613. Of these, 248 positive commandments require us to take action and 365 negative commandments require us to refrain from taking action. Some of these commandments cannot be performed now as the Holy Temple has not been rebuilt.

Many *mitzvot* are communications from people to God, such as daily prayers and lighting *Shabbos* candles. Some *mitzvot* require us to do something, such as washing our hands in a certain way and reciting particular prayers before and after eating food. Interestingly, in medieval times, when the laws of physical hygiene were not known and millions of people were dying of bubonic plague, Jews survived because of the prescribed *mitzvot* of hand washing after using the bathroom and before eating. At other times, the consumption of pork and shellfish caused health problems, but observant Jews were spared such suffering as well. The *mitzvot* do not always make sense within a logical context, but their purpose and the benefits they provide often become clear later.

Mitzvot between people include giving charity, inviting guests to your home, visiting the sick or the mourner, and refraining from *loshon hara* (malicious gossip). *Mitzvot* between people and the land of Israel allow the land to rest by letting it lie fallow every seventh year. Among the *mitzvot* between people and animals is the one that mandates eating only animals that have been slaughtered in a way that does not cause them pain. Rabbi Zalman Schachter-Shalomi, the spiritual head of the Jewish Renewal movement, coined the term "eco-kosher" to remind us that we have a responsibility to be committed to all organisms and the environment. For example, though the Torah does not stipulate that we should recycle beverage bottles, it is a *mitzvah* to do so because recycling helps the environment and we are responsible for caretaking the earth God entrusted to us. Interestingly, the Hebrew word for "man" is *adam* and for "earth" is *adamah*. The connection between the words teaches us that humans are a part of the earth. What we do for the earth, we do for ourselves. *Mitzvot* help us increase our self-awareness and connect with God. They also make the world a better place to live.

Some *mitzvot* are not physically based. The Rambam listed many *mitzvot* that we can do at any time and should try to do at all times. They include the following:

1. To know that there is a God, as it is said: "I am the Lord thy God" (Exod. 20:2, Deut. 6:4).
2. To acknowledge His unity, as it is said: "The Lord, our God, the Lord is One" (Deut. 6:4).
3. To love Him, as it is said: "And thou shalt love the Lord thy God" (Deut. 6:5).
4. To fear, or have awe, before Him, as it is said: "The Lord thy God shalt thou fear" (Deut. 6:13).
5. To pray to Him, as it is said: "And ye shall serve the Lord your God" (Exod. 23:25).
6. To cleave to Him, as it is said: "To Him shalt thou cleave" (Deut. 10:20).
7. To imitate His good and upright ways, as it is said: "And thou shalt walk in His ways" (Deut. 28:9).

These are perhaps the most challenging *mitzvot* because they require our constant focus. Even though we are commanded to do *mitzvot,* it is not because God needs us to do them but rather because we need to do them to be happy and realize our awesome potential.

We are encouraged to begin slowly and to fulfill mitzvot at a pace that we can integrate comfortably into our lives. Some people may be discouraged that they are not able to do all that is expected of them according to Jewish law, and then they question whether or not they should do anything at all. For example, a person might want to light *Shabbos* candles and pursue a deeper understanding and experience of *Shabbos* but may need to continue to work on Saturday. In such a case, it is better to light candles than not to do so, and I encourage my students to do what they can and to feel good about what they do. After a while, they often begin gently to stretch themselves. We cannot expect ourselves to do cartwheels if we haven't developed the muscles. People generally begin practicing *mitzvot* by increasing their awareness and observance of the Sabbath. However, I have also known others who felt more drawn to the practice of eating kosher food, and I have known others who began by saying blessings before eating, then took on other *mitzvot*. If you do not know where to begin, consult with a rabbi, or someone else, who can serve as a spiritual mentor to you.

Whatever you do, it is very important to strive to do it with full concentration and a full heart. At least for those moments, you may experience a taste of Godliness. While it is best to begin slowly, over time you will be able to increase your level of observance.

We tread a fine line between "feel good" and "feel bad" Judaism. We need to stretch ourselves to begin and then to maintain a committed spiritual discipline. Spiritual or religious discipline is challenging and may at times even feel uncomfortable, but that does not mean that it is not good for us. Yet, if we perform *mitzvot* with a sense of rote or out of obligation or because we fear the consequences of not doing them, we will come to resent the burden of *mitzvot* and will often judge others who do not bear the yoke of heaven as we do.

I feel it is unfortunate that so much animosity is engendered in the Jewish world over the interpretation of Jewish law. Emotions are strong everywhere. I ask, are these arguments "for the sake of heaven"? Judging your way as the best way, the right way for others, creates negativity and disunity. Wanting to impose "feel bad" Judaism is at the heart of religious conflicts in the Jewish community. Reb Shlomo Carlebach used to say that the religious Jews who look down on nonreligious Jews or the religious teenagers who throw stones on *Shabbos* are not loving and guarding the Sabbath as they profess. If religious Jews really loved the Sabbath, they would invite nonreligious Jews to their homes and would radiate the love of *Shabbos* in a way that would be totally irresistible. This would bring honor to God.

When we embark on a spiritual path, we sometimes feel it is meritorious to be harder and more stringent with ourselves than necessary. We have a righteous image of what a religious or spiritual person should be, and this is what we want to become immediately. We think if we make it harder for ourselves, if we are more strict, we will be better people or better Jews. We must be careful not to use religious observance as a way to judge ourselves or others harshly.

This will only reinforce low self-esteem. If we acquire a "holier than thou" attitude as a result of religious performance, we have fallen victim to the ego, the *yetzer hara,* the evil inclination. If this occurs, we must look deeply into our heart; we will see that our religious observance is often motivated by fear and guilt and not by a sincere desire to connect with the Holy One. Can we receive real enjoyment from this kind of service to God, or does God, so to speak, receive pleasure or honor from this approach to Him? Would we want someone to be with us, to do for us, out of fear and guilt? No. We want more. We want love. So does God.

Sometimes we are motivated religiously because we want to fit in with a particular social circle. In the Jewish world, various religious groups have dress codes that distinguish its members. If a person wants to belong to a sect, they must dress appropriately and maintain a certain level of observance. In certain religious circles, if you do not wear the proper dress you may not receive a *Shabbos* greeting. I have met so-called orthodox people who confided in me that they do not believe in God, they do not believe in Torah, but they like the orthodox community and its lifestyle.

If we are unaware of God's omnipresence, we may think that it is fine to act one way in public and a very different way in private. For example, we may act very religious in the synagogue but not at home. We may deceive some people, but we do not deceive God or ourselves. When we create a discrepancy between our private and public selves, we have forgotten about God. Somehow, we think— foolishly—that God does not see us when we are alone. Deuteronomy 29:28 says, "The secret things belong to the Lord, our God." God is in the deepest, most innermost places within us. If you believed for a moment that God is aware of your thoughts, your speech and your deeds at all times, how might this change you?

When religious observance is motivated by external factors, it is unlikely that it will be maintained over a long period of time, unless there are a lot of external perks to do so. Many years ago I was researching the *baal teshuva* movement and learned that approximately half the people who become religious will not remain so after five years if they have not married or found a supportive community within which to practice their Jewish observance.

As a general rule, I feel that if your religious observance does not make you feel more connected to all people, if it doesn't bring you greater happiness and fill your heart with love and compassion, something is wrong. You need to examine yourself carefully and reflect on your true motives. Meditate and ask God to draw you closer and help you to purify and heal your mind and heart. Select your teachers with care. We are careful about who we marry. We should be careful from whom we learn Torah. A former student recently called to tell me that she had been going to a Torah class and was leaving each class feeling very depressed and inadequate. She described the rabbi as a judgmental and coldhearted person. I advised her to find another teacher. This rabbi may be wonderful and inspiring to others, but he is not for her. When you find the right teachers, you feel you have found heaven. Keep looking until you find a teacher and/or friends who will inspire and love you and help you on this spiritual path. Seek the support of righteous people, *tzaddikim,* and read their books. Continue to nourish yourself with ongoing study to inspire you so that you can serve God with the proper intention.

Always remember that God wants your heart. This is one of the most important teachings of the Chassidic movement. I could write an entire book of all the stories I heard about the Baal Shem Tov in which he taught that a person with a sincere heart is prized over the person who knows all the laws, has all the knowledge, but does not yearn with his whole being to connect with God. In many ways, our time is not too different from the time of the Baal Shem Tov. Many Jews feel alienated from the religious establishment, yet they so much want to find a way to draw close to God. The messages of the Baal Shem Tov's teachings are truly relevant today. Following is one of the stories about the Baal Shem Tov.

In this story, the Baal Shem Tov meets a very sincere man who is praying all the prayers from the prayer book, but he does not know which prayers to say on which day. He desperately wants to know how to pray properly. The Baal Shem Tov takes the time to teach him when to say each prayer and in which order the prayers should be said. The man writes everything down and puts little slips of paper in the prayer book to remind him. Right after the Baal Shem

Tov leaves, a wind blows all the papers away. The man is dismayed. He runs to find the Baal Shem Tov to ask him again how he should pray. He travels quickly and finally sees the Baal Shem Tov by the riverbed. The Baal Shem Tov puts down a handkerchief and travels across the river on it.

In his eagerness and desperation to catch up with the Baal Shem Tov, the man simply copies him. He puts down a handkerchief on the water and then travels across the river on it. He finally reaches the Baal Shem Tov and tells him excitedly what happened. He asks the Baal Shem Tov to tell him again how to pray. The Baal Shem Tov asks how he got across the river. The man answers that, after witnessing the Baal Shem cross, he asked God to help him in the same way so he would catch up with the spiritual master and be taught how to pray. The Baal Shem Tov responds that he should continue to pray as he always has for God is surely with him.

Our most meaningful and exalted endeavor is to serve God for God's sake alone. This is true devotion: filling the heart with yearning and love. In another story about the Baal Shem Tov, he is asked to pray to save a child's life. As he does so, he hears a heavenly voice telling him not to intervene. "If you continue, you will lose your place in the World to Come." The Baal Shem Tov rejoices, saying, "Now I can serve God without thinking I'm earning a place in the World to Come." Of course he was given his place in the World to Come and the child was saved. So it is with everything. When we do something with pure motives, we are protected and elevated.

When appropriate, I encourage both my clients and students to commit to *mitzvot*. Generally speaking, I feel that if we are unhappy, confused or ill, we need to make a stronger connection to God. It is this connection that heals. To lessen depression, I recommend lighting *Shabbos* candles. To reduce anxiety, I recommend *tallis* and *tefillin*. If we need money, we need to give to other people. Of course, we must talk to God in our own words all the time and pray and pray and pray. If we do these simple acts with the desire to connect to God and with the recognition that these acts do connect us to God, who is the source of joy and freedom, we will begin to feel connected to God. Through these acts, we will be much happier.

8

TRANSFORMING SUFFERING

et's be real. Life hurts at times. Who has not suffered? Some people suffer more than others, but everyone knows firsthand about suffering at some point in their lives. Some of us may be able to say that we have grown through our suffering, some of us suffer with greater trust and faith than others, but we all suffer. As Ernest Hemingway wrote, "All of us are broken. It is just that some of us are stronger in our broken places than others." Rabbi Yitzchok Luria likened birth to descending into *mitzraim,* a place of constraints. Prior to this descent, the soul lives in high spiritual realms where it enjoys a more direct and expanded experience of the Divine Presence before it chooses to re-enter the physical world. Because the light of the Divine Presence is obscured in this physical world, hardship and limitations are present. Suffering is part of the human experience.

The Jewish people are no strangers to suffering. In my opinion, the Jewish people have suffered longer and greater than any other people. Throughout time, wherever we have lived, we have endured persecution, pogroms, holocausts and discrimination. Yet we have learned how to endure and thrive because of our connection to our Judaism. Our direct experience with pain and suffering and our capacity to withstand and endure as a people made us unusually sensitive to the pain of others. Indeed, the Jewish people have something to teach the world about transforming pain and suffering.

In the Bible, we receive many teachings about suffering. We read stories about Abraham and Sarah, Isaac and Rebecca, and Jacob going "down" to Egypt. The Hebrew word for Egypt means "narrowness" or "constraints." The Jewish people lived in Egypt for 210 years. The Bible says that God first revealed Himself to Moses in a thornbush. The *midrash,* part of the oral tradition of Judaism, asks, "Why did God choose to reveal Himself in the lowliest tree, a tree which bears no fruit?" It is said that God did so to impart to us a most important teaching. By revealing Himself in a thornbush, God told us that He is there with us in the most humble, painful places of our lives. If God had revealed Himself in a beautiful apple tree, we would think God is found only in beauty. Though it may be easier to experience Godliness in beauty or when things are going well, people often have to suffer before they can turn to God in a real way. Sometimes, we literally have to be brought down to our knees before we ask God to help us. When we realize that our efforts will not bear fruit on our own, we know that we truly need God and will call out with a whole heart for a new way. When our usual ego defenses have been shattered and we experience ourselves as empty and broken with nowhere to turn, then there is space for God to enter.

God said to Jacob, who embodies the collective soul of Israel, "I will go down to Egypt with you." With those words, God is saying to us, "When you are in a contracted place, I am also contracted and I am with you." We do not suffer alone. God suffers with us. This is a demonstration of total compassion. God is willing to be with us in our pain. As we learned in chapter 3, God contracted Himself, withdrew His Light, to create a space for something else to exist. All evil, all pain and suffering come from this original contraction and concealment. Because God's Light is concealed, we feel that we exist, that we have free will and that we can make a difference in our lives and in the lives of others. With the gift of free will, God gives us the opportunity to be creative. This is a great joy and delight. God did not want us to be puppets but to be partners. God knows that we feel better about ourselves when we feel we have made choices.

If God was just a giver and we were just recipients, we would not feel good about ourselves. Our lives would not have much meaning because there would be nothing for us to contribute. By making an imperfect world, God gives us the opportunity to perfect the world and perfect ourselves. This is similar to the analogy of a parent and a child. The parent could easily do everything for the child. It might even be easier and safer, but the child would not learn to do for himself. When the parent refrains and allows the child to learn to do for himself, the child feels happy and proud. Eventually the parent can entrust to the child increasing responsibility for himself and others. Similarly, God could do everything for us, but then what would we do? In effect, God ties His hands so we can experience a partnership with Him. God shares His power with us.

Suffering is the price we all pay for the gift of free will. Because we have free will, we can make good or bad choices. God's wisdom dictates that it is worth the gamble, even though we have to suffer because of our bad choices. God sends His Presence, *Shechinah,* to be with us. She suffers with us. It must be painful for God to watch us suffer senselessly. How much does God suffer from seeing us devote myriad resources to nuclear and biological warfare that destroy His Creation when we could have used the same resources to feed the world and eradicate disease? God's desire is for each of us to receive the deepest goodness, greatest love and highest God-revelation. God does not want us to suffer. Why should we blame God for our bad choices? God does not punish us. God suffers with us.

Why have the Jewish people suffered so much? This is a deep question, with many mysteries and inadequate answers. In almost every generation, the Jewish people have been persecuted. People often ask, if God is so powerful, how did He allow the Holocaust to occur? How can a person believe in a personal God after the Holocaust? Many people have turned away from Judaism because of this horrific catastrophe. Though explanations for the Holocaust can be found, Elie Wiesel, recipient of the Nobel Peace Prize in 1986 and author of a number of books about the Holocaust, provided a powerful response in an article published by the *New York Times.* He wrote to God, "Where were you, God of kindness, in Auschwitz? What was going on in heaven at the celestial tribunal, while your children were marked for humiliation, isolation, and death only because they were Jewish." He then presented some of the standard rationalizations given to explain the Holocaust, such as "God knows what He is doing" or "The Jewish people were being punished for their sins of assimilation." He ended the article saying, "I reject all these answers. At one point I began wondering whether I was not being fair with You. After all Auschwitz was not something that came down from heaven. It was conceived by men, implemented by men, staffed by men. And their aim was to destroy not only us but You as well. Ought we not to think of your pain, too? Watching your children suffer at the hands of your other children, haven't You also suffered?"

I would like to share with you the traditional Jewish and kabbalistic understandings of suffering, which, surprisingly, resemble much New Age thought and therapy. I hope that this information will help you endure and transform your personal suffering. By sharing these ideas, I do not want to rationalize or intellectualize the pain you may feel. When we are in the midst of pain, we need the compassion of the heart rather than explanations of the mind. If we are in pain, it is foolish to deny it or masquerade our feelings. We simply need to learn how to be with our pain, without inflicting additional unnecessary pain upon ourselves.

Too often, people feel sad or guilty about being sad, rather than feeling their original sadness. This leads to shame, depression or anxiety that may be far worse than the original pain. If you are sad, allow yourself to feel sad. If you are in pain, take deep breaths and feel your pain. Share your pain with God and with others. We know from experience that when we share our pain with others and they share theirs with us, we become bonded to them in a deep way. Similarly, when we share our suffering with God, we become bonded and united with God.

It is good to cry to God. The Talmud says that tears open the gates of heaven. Pray for healing. God is the ultimate healer. Ask others to pray for you as well. (In my book *Everyday Kabbalah,* I offer particular meditations and teachings to help cope with different kinds of pain.)

When the pain has lessened and we can begin to think more

clearly, as part of our healing we will want to make sense of what we have experienced. In *Man's Search for Meaning,* Viktor Frankl wrote about his experiences and observations of life in a concentration camp and reminded us that the worst pain can be endured if a person can find meaning and hope. If we can find meaning in our experience, we will be able to transform our suffering so that it is a positive asset in our life. Many people find God and become better people through their personal suffering.

The first thing the Talmud advises us to do when we suffer is to scrutinize ourselves because most suffering is the consequence of our own thoughts, speech and actions. Through these acts, we hurt ourselves, we hurt others and we hurt God, so to speak. We suffer mostly because of our own negativity. We create most of our own suffering. Our pain informs and motivates us to examine ourselves, to identify the thoughts, speech and actions that are causing the negativity, and to make the necessary changes. Pain is often a blessing, a wake-up call. It lets us know that something is wrong. Rather than blame yourself for creating pain, listen to it and hear the messages and lessons it offers you.

Being able to identify the connection between our actions and our suffering is a great spiritual gift. This insight is the first step in transformation. We see that negativity has come back directly or perhaps indirectly to us, and we are suffering the consequences. When we recognize that our actions—or nonactions—are the source of our suffering, it is wonderful because we can change and act differently in the future. For example, consider a person who is a diabetic. If this person continues to eat huge amounts of sugar, disregarding the doctor's advice, and becomes sick, can he reasonably blame God for his sickness? Realistically, he needs to look at his diet and his lifestyle and make the necessary changes in order to feel better.

When we are physically ill, we need to carry out a comprehensive investigation of our lifestyle and habits and consider whether something we are doing is contributing to our illness. Today we know a lot about the causes of illness. Research proves that diet, nutrition, emotional stress and environmental factors play roles in our well-being. It is our responsibility to make sure that our bodies, minds and souls are given the proper nourishment that we need for health.

I recently worked with a depressed woman who suffered tremendously from migraine headaches. She was often totally debilitated and in bed with an ice pack on her head, taking dangerously toxic pain medication every two hours. She came to see me for spiritual counseling and meditation instruction. She wanted to believe in God, but she questioned God's existence. If God existed, why did He make her suffer? She felt God must be punishing her, and inwardly she felt angry at Him.

As I do with all my clients, I inquired about her diet and made suggestions. Surprisingly, the doctor who was treating her for migraines never inquired about her diet. He had put her on very toxic headache medication that had horrific side effects. She told me that she was a sugar, chocolate and caffeine junkie. All these substances are known to contribute to migraine headaches. I told this woman that she should regard sugar and chocolate as poison and immediately stop eating them. When she changed her diet according to my recommendations and learned to breathe and meditate properly, the headaches that had plagued her for years disappeared. It was not that God was punishing her or making her suffer, but rather it was a wake-up call that she needed to live a more natural, healthy lifestyle. (Personally, I find it unconscionable that some doctors still treat illness without considering the role that diet may play. In addition, I believe it is essential that people become knowledgeable about their illnesses and not give their power away to doctors.)

In some cases, however, it is not so clear why we suffer. We have made all the changes we can, yet we continue to suffer physically and emotionally. We may consider that our suffering is a form of purification. The reason for it may become clear after self-reflection. It is possible that if we are hurt by others, we have hurt others in the very same way. For example, people who find that they have been robbed or are a victim of slander may find, after reflection, that sometime in their life they stole or committed slander against another person. It is said that sometimes people are victims of theft because they failed to give an appropriate amount to charity. They were allotted a certain amount of money by God. They were supposed to give ten percent of this sum to charity. Failing to do so, the money was taken away through robbery, stock market losses or medical expenses. If we believe there is nothing we have done, we can reflect on why we allow ourselves to be hurt by others, and we need to forgive ourselves. Our suffering is a call to carefully examine our behavior, as well as to consider the role our deep-seated subconscious motivations may have played in creating this event.

Sometimes we suffer not because of anything we have done but because we need to expand our concept of who we are. Our egos have been bruised. We may feel jealousy or any number of negative emotions. We need to develop ourselves and realize that we are not just this limited small self. We are great beings, but something may be taken away from us because we need to learn how to be more resourceful, self-reliant or compassionate. We need to learn to let go, to learn to be with ourselves in a loving way and open to God's unconditional and awesome love. Trust in God that good will come from this challenge.

Much of the suffering we experience is self-imposed. This does not mean that it is not real. Many of us grew up in dysfunctional families where we received messages quite early in our lives that we were not good enough and not lovable, that our feelings were not valid. As a result, we have formed negative ideas of who we are. We have low self-esteem regardless of how successful we have been in our lives. We tend to be self-critical and self-blaming, and we often find ourselves involved in relationships and in situations where these limiting ideas of self are reinforced, making us targets for exploitation. It will empower us to recognize that we have created much of our suffering by our own negative thoughts. Fortunately, we can change our thoughts. We have to be careful that we do not get stuck blaming ourselves. Blaming ourselves boomerangs, coming back to hurt us and making it very hard to change. Blaming others for our suffering keeps us feeling like victims, powerless and helpless. Blaming God for our pain is foolish, because it prevents us from receiving the healing that is available if we remain open to it.

One of my therapy clients had endured a difficult and painful childhood. She was so neglected that she was ten years old before it was discovered she was almost completely deaf. Unable to hear well as a child, she lived in the vivid but lonely world of her own imagination. As an adult, she found herself in relationships with men who did not listen to her and she rarely voiced her needs. At first she blamed the men, then she blamed herself for remaining in painful and unsatisfactory relationships for as long as she did. I cautioned her not to blame herself. Blaming only kept her feeling powerless and stuck in a victim pattern. She learned that she had created these relationships because they mirrored a need within herself and that she did not need to feel guilty or ashamed about this; rather, she could choose to be compassionate with herself. She stayed in these relationships because she had something to learn. And when she mastered the lessons, she graduated to other challenges.

More and more I see that we have to let go of blaming others or ourselves, completely, if we are to grow and open to greater joy in our lives. Because we have been given a pure soul, and free will, we need not be stuck in old patterns. By acknowledging the role that we may have played in creating our suffering and the growth opportunity the suffering provided to us, we can begin to allow more light into our lives. A popular New Age concept is that we have in our lives exactly what we project. To a large extent, what happens to us reflects what is occurring within us. Whether we want to acknowledge it or not, we actually have in our lives exactly what we are capable of receiving. Yet we also have free will, and we can choose to think and do differently. To heal our limiting self-concepts, we need to go beyond the mind and access the compassion within ourselves for the ways in which we have been hurt and have hurt ourselves. Compassion, not judging, allows the healing process to occur. Be compassionate with yourself when you are suffering. YHVH, the most prominent name of God, is associated with the energy of compassion. First and foremost, God is compassionate.

The Talmud says that those in prison cannot know freedom. They first need to connect with something that is free. Our relationship with God is a powerful transforming agent for personal change, enabling us to love ourselves and transcend limiting self-concepts. Real freedom is inner freedom. Only God can truly free us for only God is truly free. Through prayer, meditation, learning Torah and kabbalah, and doing *mitzvot* we become more attuned to receive the love and support we need to move forward in our lives. When we identify the roots of our suffering, we will need to do some deep healing through the process known as *teshuvah* (see chapter 9) and through the practice of affirmation (see chapters 6 and 10). Suffering is clearly part of God's plan for our perfection.

After we have done an extensive investigation into the causes of our suffering and can find nothing that would warrant this kind of pain, we may be experiencing an "affliction of love." Jewish doctrine says that sometimes we suffer not because of wrong actions but because it is through suffering that we will develop and manifest certain qualities of the soul that we would not or could not do otherwise. God gives tests and trials to people who can grow through them. God only sends afflictions of love to the people who will be able to use suffering as an opportunity for growth. As a therapist, I encounter so many people who have endured tremendous, mind-baffling hardships and childhood abuse. Much of the suffering they have endured is not because they deserved or created it. Perhaps it is because they are special souls.

I like to think that some of the extraordinary suffering I experienced in life was not because I deserved or created it but because God gave me a gift to become a better person. I do know that, having suffered, I am a much better therapist and a better spiritual teacher than I might have been had my life been easy. I am stronger and more accepting of myself and others. My suffering brought me the spiritual gifts of empathy and humility, as well as a wealth of knowledge about healing and personal growth. I am not afraid to be with people in their deepest pain, whatever their pain is, because I know that place myself. Through my trials I have been given the gift of a deeper and more powerful connection to God and can help people access their connection to God when they don't feel that they have one. So I have to acknowledge and feel grateful that there have been fruits from my suffering, though I would not consciously have chosen to suffer.

Many people who have suffered greatly attest that they become better people as a result. We may not see the gifts of our suffering when the suffering is most acute. We often need the perspective of time to see the growth that may have occurred within us. For many people, suffering holds the key to uncovering their life purpose. I have seen many individuals who changed their lives because of the

suffering they went through. They found new jobs, new relationships, a new appreciation for the simple things. They became more
in tune with themselves and what they needed in life.

I worked at a psychiatric clinic for almost two years with a very
bright and charming non-Jewish couple who experienced terrible
misfortune: Their son committed a heinous crime. This was a
tremendous trauma for them. Their lives will never be the same.
They suffered greatly because of this event on many different levels.
Though the son did not feel guilty for the crime, the parents felt
guilty and blamed themselves. When married people are in this kind
of pain, there is a tendency to blame each other. I told both of them
early in their therapy that this crisis would either take a tremendous
toll on each of them personally, perhaps even costing them their
marriage, or strengthen them individually and bond them together
in a more powerful way than before.

Through therapy they learned new ways to listen and support
each other's feelings. Their marriage actually improved. They
became much closer to each other and to their children. A new
spiritual world opened up for them. With counseling, they developed
a prayer life with each other that was very meaningful to both of
them. They prayed, meditated and said psalms together. They went
on numerous spiritual retreats, which they had never done before.
They enlisted a whole network of people to pray for their son. To
help their son physically as well as spiritually, they reached out and
connected with the highest and holiest people in the Christian community. The famous Sister Helen, known for ministering to people
on death row, took up their cause. Many miracles occurred for them.
God became a very powerful force in their recovery, and they
became better, more conscious people than they were before.

If you look into the lives of people who have made an unusual
contribution to helping others, you most often will find that they
have endured great personal suffering. Suffering motivates us to be
compassionate and committed to alleviating the pain of others. Most
spiritual healers have had life-threatening illnesses. Suffering forces
us to look more deeply into ourselves and to set different priorities
for our lives. If we believe that we can use our suffering for our own
growth, we can actually convert something we experienced as

negative to something positive. Suffering has a purpose. There are levels of spiritual clarity and purification available through suffering. As it is written in the Talmud, the olive does not give oil unless it is squeezed.

Each day, traditional prayers remind us that God rescued us and took us out of Egypt. Each day, I say the following words from the morning service in the prayer book: "Open wide your mouth and state your desires for I am the God who took you out of Egypt." When I say this, I often take a few moments to actually open my mouth like a baby ready to suck her mother's breast. I recommend you do this as well. It is a wonderful experience. Every day, we need to solicit divine assistance to take us out of Egypt and help us to be free of all that limits us.

Rabbi Nachman of Breslov said that people should realize they are helpless to alleviate their suffering on their own. Rather than running away from God at this time, which people often do when in pain, we should turn to Him, the only one who can deliver us from suffering. Though Rabbi Nachman preached a message of joy to his followers, he himself was no stranger to suffering. In his short lifetime of only thirty-eight years, he experienced the deaths of his wife, his son and his daughter-in law. He himself was continually ostracized by Jewish communities and had to move several times. Perhaps it was through his suffering that he became a very great teacher. Though Rabbi Nachman lived in the 1700s, he has more followers today than when he was alive. For thousands of Jews all over the world, Rabbi Nachman is very much alive and a personal guide and teacher to them.

Most great spiritual teachers within Judaism have attested that God is the only force to make things happen in this world. Though these men have been deeply traditional, their teachings, interestingly enough, resonate with the New Age spiritual paradigm if we keep in mind that God is inside and outside of us. It may often appear that people are operating independently, that they have free will, but this is an illusion. Other people do not hurt you. This is a hard concept to really grasp, but when we do, we are empowered. We are no longer victims of outside forces.

In his book *Duties of the Heart,* Bachya Ibn Paquda said, "No one can help or hurt another person without God's permission." When we are suffering, we should cry out to God, acknowledging that our suffering comes from God and that only God can help us. If we believe that our suffering comes from God, there must be goodness to extract from it. We should strive to find the divine message in our suffering and realize that it is our very own soul that is crying out and expressing itself through the painful circumstances that are occurring. Everything, even our pain and suffering, happens to take us forward. Listen to the message within your pain. It is your pain; let it talk to you and teach you.

If we are stubborn and blame circumstances or others for our suffering, our heart will harden like Pharaoh's did, and we will fail to see what there is for us to learn in our difficult situation. We will become increasingly disempowered. The Rambam (Maimonides) said, "It is a positive commandment of the Torah to scream out to God when any kind of sorrow, potential danger befalls us as a people. When the enemy threatens us, blow the shofar." He said that we do this to remind us that God is the source of what is happening and that all the events occurring are not coincidental.

In his book of teachings, *Ha Sulam: The Ladder,* Rabbi Yehuda Leib Ashlag, a modern-day kabbalist, said that when someone does something to you, you should think that God did it to you. Receive it with love and know that God does everything for the good of a person. Believe that this is so even though your mind may say that it cannot be so. When we suffer, we may cleave to the negativity or to the one who caused the descent. If we cleave to the one who produced the negativity, we cleave to God. By acknowledging and cleaving to God in suffering, God will take us out of the negativity. Rabbi Ashlag said because we are blinded by self-love, we cannot see this truth. If we could see through the eyes of God, we would know these secrets and we would not suffer.

I recently heard an amazing story about a man who demonstrated these teachings, a righteous person who lived in Nazi Germany before World War II. Though we may not approach the spiritual level of this person, this story may inspire you as it does me to see God's hand in whatever is happening to us.

Before the Holocaust began, the Nazis found ways to humiliate

Jews publicly. One way was to make religious Jewish men sweep the streets with their beards. One of these men was a rebbe who was blessed to survive the Nazis and live the remainder of his life in Israel. When his followers observed their rebbe sweeping the street with his beard, they sensed that he did so with a sense of equanimity.

"How can you do this, sweep the streets and look like you are enjoying yourself?" they asked him.

The rebbe replied, "At first I was upset, but then I told myself that these streets do not belong to the Nazis but to God. If the street is God's street, it is actually a privilege to clean the street with my beard."

Many years later, someone saw the rebbe sweeping the streets with his beard late at night in Tel Aviv. When he asked the rebbe why he did such a thing, the rebbe responded, "I had asked God that when I was sweeping the streets in Germany with my beard that I be blessed to do this *mitzvah* in God's streets in the Holy Land. I am simply fulfilling my promise to God." Once he was discovered, however, he stopped doing it. Some *mitzvot* can only be done in private.

Another major reason that people suffer is because of past-life karma. Reincarnation is a popular idea in New Age movement. Past-life regression therapy has now become popular. Dr. Brian Weiss, former head of psychiatry at Mount Sinai Hospital, has written a number of books about how he has regressed some of his patients to remember their past lives and how they have been healed as a result. Judaism also teaches that reincarnation explains some of the suffering we experience. (Also see chapter 13.) Sometimes we suffer in this lifetime to pay back the debts of former lives. Our souls actually choose to incarnate, to fix the wrongs we committed during a previous lifetime. Infants and children who die young may have righted many of their past-life wrongs, which may be why their lives are so short. The Lubavitcher Rebbe said that we should talk about reincarnation now because it provides a broader perspective on our lives and helps explain suffering, particularly the suffering caused by the Holocaust.

Many stories describe rebbes who knew the past lives of people and what they needed as an antidote to their suffering. In one story, a person comes to the Baal Shem Tov after experiencing a tremendous

financial setback and asks him why this happened to him. The Baal
Shem Tov tells him to go to a particular town to inquire about a man
we'll call Moshe Cohen. He goes to this town, then to the synagogue
and asks about Moshe Cohen. The people tell him that Moshe Cohen
is no longer alive but that he was infamous and will not be forgotten.
He was an informer and robbed many people of great sums of
money. In short, he was a terrible man. The man returns to the Baal
Shem Tov and asks him why he was sent to inquire about such a
despicable man. The Baal Shem Tov answers very bluntly: "You were
Moshe Cohen in your last lifetime." It is possible that some of our
suffering is because of what we did in another lifetime.

In the absence of such great rebbes, who could tell us what we
have to fix in our lifetimes, we must reflect on the times and ways
we have suffered. They indicate what we need to learn or do in this
lifetime. Suffering is actually the prime source for learning. Whether
in this incarnation or a previous one, we repeat our suffering until
we have mastered the teachings and lessons to be learned.

Sometimes a special soul is born into a difficult life because of a
decision that the soul made while in the spiritual world. The soul
does not so much need to right previous wrongs but rather wants to
demonstrate the kind of qualities that can only be seen in hardship.
A light shines more brightly in the darkness than in the presence of
light. On a deeper level, such a soul chooses to descend into the
physical world and to suffer. In this way, although the soul might not
be consciously aware of the reasons for its choice, it elevates its
position in the next world by giving encouragement and faith to
others. For example, a soul may want to demonstrate the quality of
forgiveness, compassion or faith. Because of this choice at a soul
level, the soul is placed in life situations where there will be much
opportunity to practice these qualities. As such, a person's life
serves as a model for others close to him and possibly to the world
as to how a person can maintain goodness and forgiveness in the
face of extreme adversity.

I met an extraordinary woman during a recent workshop I con-
ducted at Elat Chayyim, a Jewish spiritual retreat center in upstate
New York. Lisa was a beautiful, spiritual woman, a physician, and
was extremely environmentally sensitive. She had to wear a mask

during the program. As I got to know her during the week, it occurred to me that environmentally sensitive people or people who are sick with the new autoimmune disorders are often very special and spiritual people. At a profound level, perhaps their souls have volunteered to suffer to demonstrate to the world that the natural balance of the environment is being destroyed. Their pain is a warning to the world to change.

Another explanation given as to why people suffer is simply that it is their *mazel* (usually translated as "luck"). These people do not suffer because of anything they have done in this life or in a past life or even to learn something through suffering. They suffer because it is their *mazel*.

Judaism does embrace astrology, teaching that we are each born under a certain constellation and with a certain destiny. It is as simple as that. Our sages say that length of life, number of children and sustenance depend not on merit but on destiny (Mo'ed Katan 28a). The Talmud (Shabbos 156a) mentions many aspects of life that are determined by the constellation under which a person is born. Yet it is also said by most of the Amara'im, teachers included in the Talmud, that the nation of Israel is not subject to astrology. How does the Talmud resolve this contradiction? *Tosafos*, the commentary on the Talmud, says that it is possible through great merit to change our destiny. Rashi, the great Torah commentator, said that charity, prayer or *mitzvot* can improve our *mazel,* and this is what is meant when the Talmud says, "Jews are not subject to astrology."

However, it is not always possible to change our destiny, no matter how much effort we make. The Talmud offers an example of Rabbi Elazar ben Pedas, who was so poor that he fainted and fell asleep. In a dream vision, he asked God, "Why must I suffer in this world?" God answered, "Would you rather I should turn back to the beginning of time so you would be born under a different constellation?"

Ibn Ezra, another great Torah commentator, said that if we place our full trust in God, we will be spared from any harm predicted in our horoscope. The Rambam tells us to believe that our future depends on how close we are to God and doing His will. Though the Rambam acknowledges that the constellations have a major impact on our lives, we should not feel resigned to our fate but should always remember that we are only part of Creation and that God controls us. According to astrology, Abraham knew that he was not destined to have children with his wife Sarah. When he performed the circumcision on himself and his son Ishmael, he became worthy of bearing a son, Yitzchok, with his wife.

Even with all these explanations of why people suffer, we may still not feel them personally relevant when we, or our loved ones, are suffering. When we hear about people dying because of earthquakes, wars or terrorism, everything seems so random. It is natural that we wonder if there is order to the world. We still have questions. We ask, "Is there justice?" and "Where is God?"

Reb Shlomo Carlebach used to ask, "What is the matter with a question?" A question can be very deep. Questions do not always require answers. Some questions do not have answers. We need to listen and be with our own questions and the questions of others in a respectful way, allowing any emotion to surface as we hold a spiritual question regarding our pain or that of others. The questions we may have about why we suffer are often much deeper than any answers we come up with to explain or rationalize our pain.

Through our encounters with suffering, we learn firsthand that life is not so simple. Life is deep and mysterious. God is deep. God is real. When we are in pain, we realize that we do not control life, nor do we control God. Our pain enables us to see through illusions, to access the depths of life and to be open to the reality of God. When we do this we are given strength.

Contacting the Deepest Questions
of the Soul

Take a few deep breaths. Imagine that God is before you and you can ask any question about your life that you would like. Get in touch with the questions that are the deepest for you, those that you might be embarrassed to say out loud or to share with anyone. Now pose a question inwardly, then pose it out loud to God. Be with the question and listen to any responses that occur within you. You might want to rationalize, explain or answer the question, but quiet that tendency and allow the question to be spoken and heard deep inside. Questions do not always need answers. Be with your question and repeat it several times, accompanied by long, deep breaths. Periodically check your breath to be sure you are not holding it. There is a tendency to hold the breath to block the expression and release of emotion. Allow any emotions to surface during this process. The contacting or release of feeling is a gift. Observe it with compassion, and let it flow through you.

Record your experience.

Repeat the previous meditation, but now imagine that God shares your question, along with your pain, confusion, wonderment and yearning. For example, a typical question of a single person is "Why am I alone?" Imagine that the unification of God and the *Shechinah,* the Divine Presence, is also diminished by your feeling of deprivation. The *Shechinah* feels your pain; for example, the Gemara says that when a couple gets divorced, the *Shechinah* sheds tears.

Record your experience.

Repeat the above meditation, but now imagine that God asks the same question you just asked Him. For example, God asks, "Why am I alone?" Take note of the insights and feelings that are now evoked.

Record your experience.

Now imagine that God is compassionately reflecting your question back to you. "Why are you alone?" Take a few long, deep breaths and listen to any shifts in awareness that occur as a result of this meditation.

Record your experience.

 ## Journey to Inner Knowing

In Judaism, as in most spiritual traditions, there is a belief in the power and blessing of righteous and holy people. This belief is most prominent in Chassidic and other religious circles, but even in nonreligious circles, there is respect for people with great wisdom and accomplishment. Though Judaism emphasizes the direct connection each person has with the divine, it allows for the role of the holy person as a possible intercessor. The following exercise is included to facilitate your contacting your own inner rebbe, contacting the wisdom of your own soul. The answers to your deepest questions lie within you. This meditation will help you access them.

Take a few deep breaths and imagine yourself embarking on a journey to a wise and holy person. It may even be someone you know or a historical figure. See yourself entering into and traveling through a forest, with shafts of sunlight shining through the trees. As you walk, you become more clear about the deep, personal questions you would like to ask this holy person. Soon you come to a clearing and you see a little house that is basked in golden sunlight. You approach the house, meet this holy person and ask your question. You listen to the answer.

Record the response you hear.

9

FIXING OUR MISTAKES

The Talmud says that when we die, we appear before the heavenly court and are shown two scenarios of our lives. We are shown our life as we lived it and the life we could have lived had we not sinned. (For now, let us define sin as the separation of ourselves from divine goodness.) If the two versions of life are closely aligned, we are in heaven, having done what we were supposed to do with our life. If the versions are very different, we are in hell.

The suffering we feel after life comes from inside us, from the recognition that we damaged our own soul and our capacity to receive the goodness of God. Mercifully, throughout our lives we are given the opportunity to reconcile these two pictures of our lives through *teshuvah*. Thus, it behooves us to periodically reflect on our lives to assess whether we are living lives worthy of who we really are. Though it is never easy to do this, it is easier for us to do so while we are alive and can make changes. We need to bear in mind that we will have to face ourselves and God for what we have or have not done. While we are living, we can repair our mistakes through *teshuvah*.

We all make mistakes in life. We hurt ourselves, we hurt others and we hurt God. God is the source of goodness, yet we hold

ourselves back, we sabotage, deny, and limit our capacity to give and
receive this goodness. We bring suffering upon ourselves and others
to varying degrees. Yet none of us should say that because of our
mistakes we cannot change and become better people. The Torah
records the sin of worshipping the golden calf to demonstrate that
when the Jews did *teshuvah* for this sin, they were forgiven. They
then received the gift of the *Mishkon,* the tabernacle for the Divine
Presence in their midst.

Teshuvah is often translated as "repentance," and it literally
means "to return" or to "turn in a new direction." *Teshuvah* has
many facets. In its most common usage, it often connotes a return
to or an acceptance of a greater level of Jewish observance. It also
refers to the acknowledgment of an error, the resultant feelings of
regret, and the commitment to correct a situation and do differently
in the future. On the deepest, most mystical level, *teshuvah* is the
return to inner wholeness, beauty and potential, a return to the soul
and the memory and experience of oneness with the divine. Usually,
for *teshuvah* to be complete, it includes all aspects of the above.
Though the teachings on *teshuvah* presented here are based on a
traditional paradigm, they are relevant to us today. To be happier,
more actualized people, we need to confront our shortcomings, heal
our resentments, learn to forgive, let go and move on. The popular
Twelve-Step programs for people with all kinds of addictions are
based on principles akin to the *teshuvah* principles.

In traditional Jewish prayer, every day we ask God to help us do
teshuvah. We affirm that God wants us to do *teshuvah.* No matter
how far away we may feel from God, we can always return to Him.
Though *teshuvah* occurs throughout the year, the time period prior
to and during the High Holidays—Rosh Hashanah and Yom Kippur—
is considered most auspicious.

The Talmud says that *teshuvah* was created before the creation of
the world, even before the creation of man. The capacity for change
and transcendence was part of the original design of the world. The
capacity to do *teshuvah* is a demonstration and expression of the
divine gift of free will. It is truly a gift because it signifies that we do
not have to be bound by the limitations of the past. Our sages say

that *teshuvah* has the power to convert into positive assets all of our negative choices and experiences.

The Lubavitcher Rebbe, in *Likkutei Sichos*, asked, "How can repentance transform the sin itself, an act performed against God's Will, into a positive deed?" He answered this question by saying that in doing *teshuvah*, our sin, which originally separated us from our own soul, now motivates and directs us to establish a deeper and more powerful relationship with God. We become better people than we might have been had we not had the difficult challenges, hardships and negativity that originally propelled or coerced us into *teshuvah*. It is said that a person who masters *teshuvah*, called a *baal teshuvah*, stands in a higher place than a totally righteous person.

Reb Shlomo Carlebach told a story based on a teaching of the Rizhiner Rebbe that is a beautiful analogy of the *teshuvah* process. Imagine a man is riding in a car and stops at a traffic light, where he sees the most beautiful woman. The light changes and they both drive away. He feels badly that he lost the opportunity to ask her for her telephone number. Time passes and he accumulates a lot of parking tickets and has to go to traffic court. He waits in line, preparing his defense, feeling depressed that he has to spend his time in this way. Finally, it is his turn. He approaches the bench and to his amazement he sees that the judge is the same woman he saw in the car. How happy he is to have another chance to see her! This is similar to the process of *teshuvah*. *Teshuvah* is an opportunity to come close to God. When we are close to God, we are grateful for all the good and the bad because everything contributed to bringing us close.

Teshuvah instills and affirms a sense of responsibility for our own lives. It is not an easy process. It may feel uncomfortable to examine the ways we have as individuals and communities made choices that did not support the expression and well-being of our own soul, of the souls of others and of the divine in this physical world. Sometimes we attempt to comfort ourselves and others by saying that our life circumstances or, for example, our dysfunctional families have made us who and what we are and that we really had no choice. It is true that all these external influences have impacted who we experience ourselves to be, but if we get stuck in blaming others and ourselves, we are not able to access our capacity to transcend the external world, to connect with the divine and to reclaim our power of choice. Through *teshuvah* we come in touch with our essence and with the inner strength to express ourselves.

When we do *teshuvah,* we acknowledge and regret our sins and pledge not to repeat them. We know that we have been successful in *teshuvah* when we are placed in a similar situation and choose differently. Finally, we make penance, which rectifies the suffering we have caused. It is often not enough simply to regret what we have done; we must do something to rectify the situation.

Forgiveness is so liberating and is emphasized in New Age books. Rabbi Elimelech, a great rebbe of the eighteenth century, was known to ask for forgiveness of everyone in his household before *Shabbos* each week. He would go to each servant, each child and to his wife, begging them to forgive him for anything he might have done unintentionally to hurt them in any way. It is a good thing to routinely ask for forgiveness from people we are close to because it is very possible that we have hurt them unintentionally. People do not always share how they have been hurt.

Human beings are sensitive. We can hurt people intentionally or unintentionally, not just by our actions or our nonactions but also by our speech and even by our thoughts. Judaism gives particular emphasis to the power of speech to heal or hurt people. As God created the world through speech, in a similar manner we create our world through speech. Speech is a great gift, and we influence others in very powerful ways through our words. Therefore, we need to be particularly mindful of how we communicate. People say things in anger that they really do not mean, but their words can continue hurting long after the exchange. People gossip or slander others, unaware that they are damaging someone. This damage can be done even though the victim may not be consciously aware of what was said.

Even a careless remark in speech can wound another. It happens all the time. We may not even be aware that we have hurt someone. Just the other day an acquaintance said something to me that I imagine he felt was encouraging, but inwardly I felt that it was inappropriate and, in fact, his words were painful to me. I smiled, rather than expose my vulnerability. I was embarrassed to tell him that he hurt me, and I chose to distance myself from him. I imagine this happens more frequently than we like to admit. People can be so insensitive to the pain of other people. We need to think before we speak: Will these words comfort this person or help him to grow and feel better about his life? If the answer is no, it may be better not to say anything.

We hurt the people closest to us the most, often unknowingly and unintentionally. Parents routinely hurt their children by belittling them, calling them names and harshly admonishing them. People say hurtful things to their own children who they love deeply. Have you ever heard someone say to his child, "You are a bad boy" or "God doesn't love you when you do this"? On the streets of New York, I have heard parents say to a child "Shut up or I'll kill you" or "I wish you were dead." I do not think these people would ever consider themselves to be child abusers, but these words do take a toll. Many therapists' offices are filled with adults who were told such things by parents who really loved them.

Husbands and wives often hurt each other with insensitive remarks and a lack of appreciation for the goodness they receive from each other. Marriages provide the opportunity to heal childhood wounds, but too often couples unconsciously afflict each other with the same wounding they received as children. I see this so clearly when working with couples in marital counseling.

Even our thoughts can hurt people. We can give others "the evil eye" by being jealous of their accomplishments.

Judaism has many laws regarding *loshon hara,* evil speech, laws that, interestingly, exist for the protection of the perpetrator. We hurt other people when we speak badly of them, but we hurt ourselves even more, on many levels. It is said in kabbalah that when we speak evil about others, we create a prosecuting angel who accuses us and prevents us from receiving the good we might otherwise merit. As we talk about others, as we judge others, so we are judged in heaven. This point is also illustrated in *Ethics of the Fathers.* Akavia ben Mahalalel said, "Consider three things and you will not come into the grip of sin. Know from where you came, to where you are going, and before whom you will give justification and reckoning." The Hebrew words for justification and reckoning are *din ve chesbon,* which translate as "judgment, then accounting," even though we would expect them to mean that first we make an accounting, then we are judged. It is taught that when we die, we will be asked to make a judgment about someone else who has a situation similar to our own. I imagine we will see our own life pass before us, but we will not at first know it is our life. How we judge that person or ourselves will be how we are judged. For our own self-interest, it is best to develop compassion.

There is even a Jewish prohibition against listening to bad words about another person, even if they are true. When we say bad things about ourselves or our spouse, this is also *loshon hara.* We have to remind people to refrain from making judgments about themselves and others and to speak about their feelings. We can listen to people ventilate their pain as it is often healing for them to do so. We are also permitted to listen to negative statements about a person if the intention is to protect us in business or in making a *shidduch* (a match for marriage). Otherwise, such comments do not concern us. A person should not waste time engaging in idle gossip. Can you imagine a world where there is no *loshon hara*?

 Where Are You?

In the Bible, God called out to Adam, "Where are you?" He did so not because He did not know where Adam was but because He was giving Adam an opportunity to acknowledge his sin and repent. This primordial call from God to each of us, "Where are you?" continues to resound within the deep recesses of our being. Listening to God's call, the "small voice within," keeps us on track, gives us direction. This is the call for *teshuvah.*

There is no place to hide from God, yet we try to hide from God when we do something wrong. Everything is seen by God, even our innermost feelings and thoughts, because we are contained within God. This idea is humbling and transformational.

God knows everything because everything is a part of Him. We cannot hide anything from God or escape from Him. Everything is known by God. This awareness forces us to be conscious and responsible in ways that we otherwise would not be. The following meditation introduces the *teshuvah* process.

Take a few long, deep inhalations through the nostrils and exhale through the mouth, making a sound like a wave in the ocean. Focus on the breath, and allow your mind to quiet. When you feel more relaxed, breathe through your nostrils and follow the breath inside. Go to the place between the breaths, the quiet, empty space inside.

Listen to the first question asked of man in the Torah: "Where are you?" Ask yourself "Where am I?" To intensify this meditation, hear the question being asked to you with your Hebrew or English name. "Where are you, _____?" Imagine that this question to you is being called out from heaven with great love. Hear your name being called. Feel that you are being summoned to be fully present. Continue to follow your breath, pausing in the spaces between the breaths. In the empty, quiet space, listen and allow yourself to go deep inside to the core of your being. Go to that place where only you can go. Listen to the voice that responds "Here I am." Say to yourself "Here I am" and listen. Stay present with yourself, using the breath as a centering tool. Continue to open to the present moment and to the Divine Presence that addresses you.

THE ACTUAL WORK OF TESHUVAH

Many years ago, I self-published a book entitled *The Gift of a New Beginning* that was based on worksheets I had developed for my students years before to prepare for the High Holidays. Many individuals reported that doing the exercises outlined was extremely helpful. I know one person's marriage was greatly improved because of the *teshuvah* she did. I met a number of people who used this material for small gatherings to prepare for the High Holidays. The following material on *teshuvah* is based on this earlier book. It is not necessary to limit doing these exercises to the time around the High Holidays. *Teshuvah* is a daily process.

The following meditations are designed to start the process of reflecting on the ways you may have limited and hurt yourself and others in your action, speech and thought. Take time to reflect on the relevance of these words as you say them. It may even be helpful to write about particular episodes that come to mind during reflection. If you are unclear about what wrongs you need to right through *teshuvah*, ask the people closest to you if you might have said or done anything that hurt them.

 ## Seeking Forgiveness

You limit others. . . . You are jealous. . . . You speak *loshon hara*. . . . You hurt others intentionally or unintentionally through your thoughts, your words and your actions. . . . You fail to be there for others when you could extend yourself and make a difference. . . . You are selfish. . . . You are coldhearted. . . . You judge others in a poor light. . . . You create distance between yourself and others. . . . You lead others into negativity. . . . You are haughty. . . . You become upset when your needs are not met when and in the way you want. . . . You allow yourself to be mistreated by others. . . . You manipulate people. . . . You deceive them. . . . You feign affection to meet your own ends.

We are told to seek forgiveness directly from those we have hurt. Consider the people you may have hurt. Consider the possibility that you will be held back in your life by the hurt and resentments of the people you have hurt. Make a list of people for whom you have caused pain, and ask them for forgiveness. It is traditional to do this before Rosh Hashanah or Yom Kippur, but it can be done anytime. You need not specify the particular negative action unless you are requested to do so. Sometimes, telling a person that you spoke *loshon hara* about him or that you secretly harmed him in another way may be counterproductive. This will cause more pain.

It is easier to rectify physical wrongdoing. For example, stolen money must be repaid and followed by a confession of regret. If you caused emotional harm to another person, can you put a price tag on what you have done? If you are really sincere and want to show your true regret, you will have to demonstrate your remorse through your actions. If you were selfish, you must now be generous to an extreme; if you verbally abused someone, you must go out of your way to honor him.

It is possible that your request for forgiveness will not be accepted. When you ask for forgiveness, it is important that you make every effort to listen, to assuage hurt and anger, and to make restitution for any loss or pain that was experienced because of you. Tell the person how much you regret hurting him. If necessary, beg the person to forgive you. Speak of your commitment to do differently in the future. The Rambam recommends that you do this three times, if necessary, to obtain forgiveness. When approaching someone for forgiveness, the Rambam advises bringing three friends to constitute a makeshift Jewish court. If, after all these efforts, the person still does not forgive you, pray for his welfare and the healing of his anger and for God to open his heart to forgive you. Remember to be patient; the process of healing and forgiveness may take some time.

If you are unable to make rectification directly to others, you may want to give to charity in their name. If it is impossible to know the extent of the harm you may have caused, if you are unable to make appropriate restitution, do something for the benefit of the community at large. If you are unsure of what to do, discuss it with a rabbi.

I want to share a story about *teshuvah* that I find particularly moving. A man was unable to have children with his wife after many years of trying. He went to the rebbe to ask for a blessing. The rebbe asked him how much he wanted a child.

"More than anything in the world," the man replied.

The rebbe answered. "If you want children so much, you must take all your money and go to Leipzig as soon as possible and ask forgiveness from Miriam, the woman you were engaged to ten years ago but did not marry."

He immediately did as the rebbe told him. He was lucky, for he arrived in Leipzig during a weeklong fair that attracted people from all over the countryside. Miriam would surely be there. During the week, the man looked and looked for Miriam, but he could not find her. He put signs up everywhere. Finally, it was the last day and he was losing hope of ever finding her. Feeling hopeless and dejected, he sat down on a bench with his head in his hands. He felt so downcast. He could barely pray to God, but he did, and just as he was getting up to look for Miriam once again, a woman sitting next to him said, "Why are you leaving me again?"

In his despair, he hadn't noticed her. Now, he looked and saw that it was Miriam. He told her he came to the fair to find her and ask her forgiveness for breaking his engagement of marriage to her. She told him that she would forgive him if he brought a certain amount of money to her brother whose daughter was to be married the next day but who did not have enough money for the wedding and the dowry. If her brother did not find the money, the marriage would be off and his daughter would be ashamed and heartbroken. The money she requested was exactly the amount of money that he had left in his pocket. That was all the money he had.

The man jumped on his horse and rode all day and night. When he arrived at her brother's house, he looked like a person who had not slept or washed for days. He knocked on the door. The brother opened the door and the man told him that he had a gift from his sister—enough money to pay for the dowry and the wedding. The brother questioned him roughly and slammed the door in his face. The man cried out, "I am Abraham. I was engaged to marry your sister ten years ago. I just saw her and she asked me to give you this money."

The brother responded, "It is impossible. My sister died ten years ago of a broken heart." They both realized that Miriam had come from the next world to give Abraham an opportunity to do *teshuvah* and save her niece from humiliation.

When Reb Shlomo Carlebach told this story one day, a man in the audience admitted to him that he had also broken his engagement with a woman who had been devastated by her loss. At that time the man and his wife were unable to have a child. Fortunately, the other woman was still alive, and he found her and asked for forgiveness. When she gave it, he and his wife conceived a child.

If you can obtain forgiveness directly from the person you have hurt while this person is alive, you have been given a great gift. In the case of someone who died before you had a chance to ask for forgiveness, the Rambam suggests you go with ten people to the person's grave, confess your sin publicly and say, "I sinned against God, the Lord of Israel, and against this person by _____ (state what you did)."

FORGIVING OTHERS

Reflect on the ways you have suffered or been hurt by other people. The Bible says, "You should not hate your friend in your heart" (Lev. 19:17). Are there people you cannot forgive for the hurt they caused you? If you are unable to forgive them, you have a responsibility to tell them how they hurt you and how they could have treated you differently. This is actually an act of kindness on your part, for you are giving them an opportunity to do *teshuvah*. You may prevent future suffering by doing so. When you tell someone that he has hurt you, be sure to do so in a way that honors, respects and empowers him to be a better person. It is a good idea to begin a criticism of a person's behavior with a compliment. For example, "I know that you are a very sensitive and caring person, but I was hurt when you. . . ." Tell him in a calm, gentle manner how you have been hurt. If you are angry, wait for the anger to subside. Expressing yourself when you are angry with angry words will only escalate the situation. Be careful not to label the person. He is not a bad person. He just did things that were bad. Speak specifically and directly about the behavior that hurt you. Rather than make accusations, state how you feel, beginning your statements with the words "I feel."

If you would like to forgive and establish a harmonious relationship and need to receive something more than an apology, state that as well. Often an apology will not be sufficient if you have been badly hurt. It is best that the suggested restitution come directly from the perpetrator, but you may request what you feel is appropriate. If the matter cannot be resolved, seek a mutual friend or a professional mediator or a trained rabbi or a rabbinical court to mediate for you.

If you have told your friend about your pain and he continues to be insensitive to your feelings, it may be necessary to distance yourself and pray for healing and the ability to forgive him. We must make an effort to forgive others who have hurt us. It is primarily an act of compassion we do for ourselves. It is not always easy to forgive when we have been deeply hurt, but carrying anger inside hurts us more. It keeps us feeling like victims, wounded with all kinds of hurt feelings that in turn reinforce a limiting sense of who we are. When we forgive another, we are essentially forgiving ourselves for allowing this negative situation to occur. We recognize our own responsibility for what has occurred. If we stew in our anger and hurt, we become immobilized emotionally and are unable to open to the new opportunities that life offers us each day. It helps to forgive by reflecting on what the person must have felt inside to mistreat you in such a way. Usually people who hurt others have themselves been hurt. We also have to explore and acknowledge how we may have contributed to the pain we have experienced. We may have made ourselves inappropriately vulnerable. We should consider that God is using this pain to teach us something about ourselves and life, strengthening us and our connection to Him.

FORGIVING OURSELVES

In addition to doing *teshuvah* to others, we also need to do *teshuvah* for ourselves. We hurt ourselves probably more than we hurt others. God created each of us with a beautiful soul and body, yet we do not always live our life with this awareness. We sometimes place ourselves in situations that dishonor us.

Please use the following to assist you in your personal *teshuvah* process. As you say these words, reflect on their personal relevance to you.

Forgiving Oneself

You limit yourself . . . . You are angry. . . . You are depressed. . . . You think too much of yourself. . . . You think too little of yourself. . . . You worry needlessly. . . . You fail to nourish the beautiful soul within you. . . . You dragged this soul into all kinds of experiences that stifled and imprisoned her. . . . Do you listen to the needs of your soul?. . . You mistreat your physical body, the temple of your soul. . . . You do not eat the most nourishing foods. . . . You fail all too often to provide your body with adequate rest or exercise. . . . You overindulge in sensual pleasures and acts of sexual impurity.

The antidote to negativity is positive affirmation. Affirm that you will honor yourself as a special, holy, unique, worthy person who God has created to love and be loved. In hurting other people and ourselves, our real sin lies against God who created us for goodness. We will still have to answer to God ultimately, even if the people we have hurt forgive us. God created this world to bestow goodness and gave us life and so many gifts. Mostly He gave us the opportunity to create a dwelling place for Him in this world, yet what do we really do to bring Godliness to this world?

As part of your *teshuvah* process, it is important that you make a commitment to nurture and strengthen your connection to the goodness of life and to God Himself. This will be your greatest protection against negativity and harm to yourself and others. You may want to do another *mitzvah* to strengthen and protect you from doing wrong or perform an act of lovingkindness for another person or for yourself. And it goes without saying that meditation and prayer are the best tonics for the soul.

10

BEING A MORE LOVING PERSON

Love in the modern world is confusing and elusive for many people. Fifty percent of marriages end in divorce. Of those who stay married, only a small percentage have loving marriages. Many married people live very independently from each other—"married single," as one of my students calls it. As a psychotherapist, I see many couples who have remained in horrendous marital relationships. Also, there are many more single people today who are either resigned to or disappointed about being single. It is disconcerting. People are very accomplished, educated and successful in their careers, but unhappy and unsuccessful in their love lives.

Today, in many ways, people have greater opportunity to love than ever before. In the past, marriages were often financial arrangements. People stayed married because they could not afford not to be. Today, men and women are more financially independent and can marry not because they have to but because they want to love. Today, men and women want love and intimacy very much, but they wonder how to have the intimate loving relationships they want. As we move more into the New Age, our capacity to have truly loving and intimate relationships with others will become even more important to us.

Judaism has always recognized the importance of love. Within its vast reservoirs of teachings stretching back to ancient times, it offers much relevant and profound guidance to the modern world about what love is and how people can become more loving.

A story is told of a non-Jew who goes to Hillel, a great Jewish sage of the first century B.C.E., and asks him to teach him the entire Torah while standing on one foot. Hillel replies, "The essence of the Torah is this: Do not do unto anyone what you would not want done unto you. The rest is commentary." There are many things that are interesting about this succinct advice. First, we might expect that Hillel, being one of the greatest Jewish sages, would say that the essence of Torah would be loving God or doing His will or learning or keeping the Ten Commandments. Rather, Hillel said that the essence of Torah is treating other people the way you want to be treated. How simple and yet how profound!

It is also interesting that Hillel stated this wise axiom in the negative. Hillel most likely knew that people may profess words of love and even on occasion do many loving things, yet also be capable of negative and harmful thoughts and actions when it suits them. Hillel's advice asks us to consider other people before we act and to be careful not to harm another person. We need to reflect, to empathize, to imagine ourselves in another's place and to consider whether our actions would hurt another. Would we be hurt if we were in another's place? This kind of consideration and thoughtfulness is the foundation of Torah. It is the first step. We must first learn how to restrain ourselves from fulfilling our own personal desires if these needs will hurt someone else in the process.

Abraham, the forefather of multiple religions, was considered the embodiment of lovingkindness. The *midrash,* the oral teachings, say that Abraham's tent did not have walls so that he could see who was coming from every direction and run out to help them. In the Bible, it is recorded that Abraham had a visitation from the *Shechinah,* the Divine Presence, to comfort and heal him after his circumcision when he was one hundred years old. During this time, three strangers approached his tent and he chose to leave the ecstasy of his direct experience with the *Shechinah* to tend to their needs.

Thus, we learn from Abraham that loving other people means

putting aside your own spiritual experience to meet their needs. This theme is reiterated in many Chassidic stories. In one of my favorite tales, Rabbi Levi Yitzchok Berdichover failed to arrive at synagogue for services on Yom Kippur, the holiest day of the year. People had traveled great distances for the privilege of being with the rebbe. Unwilling to begin without him, the congregation waited and waited. After some time, they went out looking for him. They found the rebbe caring for a newborn baby who had been left home alone while the parents hurried to be at the synagogue for the Kol Nidre prayer. The parents thought it was more important to be at Yom Kippur services than to take care of their little baby. The rebbe thought it was more important to tend to the baby, to be there to comfort him if he woke up.

The Bible, the Talmud and Chassidic stories communicate to us that nothing is more important than loving and caring for other people. This is truly the highest service, what God wants. Through loving other people, you become close to God in a very direct way. Closeness is measured by resemblance. As God gives, so you become like Him when you give. When you do good, when you do God's Will, God is there with you, whether you feel Him or not.

Rabbi Akiva, one of the central rabbinic figures of the Talmud, went further than Hillel and preached that the essence of Torah is "Love your neighbor as yourself." This is the perfect balance. We should love ourselves, but not at the expense of others. We should love others, but not at the expense of ourselves. Most importantly, this statement implies that we must first love ourselves before we can really love others.

How do we truly love ourselves? What is the basis for loving ourselves? I feel that loving ourselves cannot be based on our talents. If I say that I love myself because I am an intelligent, handsome or even a good person, I am not loving myself. Such love is conditional. True love is essentially unconditional. I believe that loving ourselves begins with the recognition that God created us in His image and likeness and that God loves us unconditionally. To truly love myself, I must allow myself to be vulnerable before God and open to His ever-flowing, everlasting, unconditional love. To receive this love, we need to create channels within ourselves and our lives by meditating and doing good things for ourselves and others. It is not selfish to love and nurture ourselves. It is the essential foundation for loving relationships with others.

All too often, people seek relationships in which they are loved by others before they have learned to love themselves. Such relationships often are challenging, painful and addictive. If we are not loving to ourselves, we often create relationships that are not loving to us. I just had a counseling session with a woman who expressed deep feelings of loneliness and despair about ever finding a man to love her. She is beautiful, brilliant, delightful, charming and financially independent. I think she is a great "catch." She has a pattern of calling me for crisis intervention when a relationship with another unavailable man is ending. Over the years, I have encouraged her to develop a loving, intimate relationship with herself, whether she is in a relationship with a man or not. During the times when she is in not in a relationship with a man, rather than being depressed and anxious about this, she could be grateful because God has provided her with the opportunity and time to heal and love herself. As she heals and learns to love herself more, she will be naturally attracted to men who love themselves and who will love her. Our relationships with others often reflect our relationship with ourselves. Unless we love ourselves, we will not be able to give and receive love from others.

We experience many forms of love in our lives. We learn how to give and receive love in the intimacy of our family relationships. If we have not learned it there, we will need to do remedial work in therapy, in prayer and meditation to learn how to truly love. The following meditation offers a way to increase the capacity to love ourselves. I often do a variation of this meditation in my private practice as a psychotherapist.

 Meditation to Love Yourself

Take a few deep breaths to center yourself. With each inhalation, allow yourself to open and expand. With each exhalation, allow yourself to release stress, exhaling first through the mouth. When you are most centered, exhale through the nose and follow your breath inside. With each exhalation, go deeper inside yourself. Let your mind quiet. Imagine yourself as an empty vessel, ready to receive luminous, white, loving, healing light flowing into your vessel. This is the light of love. This light pours in through the top of your head, passing to the neck, shoulders, and through the entire body, the torso, arms, buttocks, legs. Fill yourself with this light. Feel the light of love within you and surrounding you. . . . Feel yourself in the presence of God.

Consider these words of the prophet Isaiah: "I have loved you with an everlasting love." This "I" is God. God's love is unconditional and everlasting. Be open to the possibility that you are loved unconditionally. Keep breathing and opening to this deepest truth that you are loved. Give yourself a hug. Allow yourself to be hugged on all levels of being. This hug is an expression of your willingness to be nurtured and to nurture yourself physically, emotionally and spiritually. Feel that you are being embraced by God. Breathe in this love for a few minutes.

Now see an image of the child you once were. How old are you? Does this child know that he or she is loved unconditionally? It is likely you did not receive this important message, but you can now give this message to the child who still lives inside you. Tell this child "I love you. God loves you." Does this child believe you? If not, tell the child "I love you" again and again. Go deeper inside and find this unconditional love. Tell the child "I love you and always will." Tell the child you will be there in the easy times and the hard times, in the good times and the bad times. Carry the child in your arms to the healing light with which you have just been filled.

Now imagine that instead of growing up feeling hurt and frightened, you knew that you were loved unconditionally. Review your life and allow God's Light and love to heal the broken places inside you. You made decisions early in life to cut off parts of yourself that you felt were not acceptable. You may have felt that you were unlovable or not good enough. Look at yourself now through the eyes of love and compassion. Can you love and accept this child as she or he is? See yourself at ten years old in this child. Take this child to your heart and surround the child with your unconditional love. Tell this child that God loves her. See yourself at twenty years of age and love yourself.

See yourself as you are now, basking in God's Light and unconditional love, with trust and faith in His goodness. What does your life look like through the awareness of God's unconditional love? Allow some images and situations to float through your mind. What new possibilities emerge for you? Breathe in these images that allow the magnificent and joyful, pure and precious soul that you are to be more fully expressed in your life. Bring your awareness back to the present moment.

There are many references to love in the Bible. We are commanded to love. The Torah says numerous times, "Love the stranger." The Torah says, "Love God with all your heart and soul" and "Love your neighbor as yourself." In response, people often ask, "Can we be commanded to love?"

Love is a feeling. Can we be commanded to feel something? We either feel something or we don't. However, the Torah would not have commanded us to feel something if it were not possible. The Alter Rebbe, Rabbi Schneur Zalman of Lubavitch, responded to this question at length in *Tanya,* his masterpiece. In essence, most of the book is a response to the question of how to love God. The rebbe recommended that we train ourselves to realize that everything we see is the outer garments of God. Everything was created by God. God is within everything and everyone, animating and sustaining all reality. When we penetrate the underlying reality of life, we are naturally filled with love and gratitude for God. He also said that by learning Torah and doing God's Will, a person will be brought to love naturally. The head of a person is located higher than the heart because what we think influences what we feel. By thinking proper thoughts, we arouse the heart to love.

In the heart and soul of every person is a deep and awesome

capacity for love, implanted by God Himself. God wanted to love and be loved. It was for this reason that He created this world. Similarly, the deepest desire within a person is to love and be loved. We were created to love and we create through love. Love is integral to our being. It is the fabric of our lives. Loving is natural. When we love, we are in touch with the essence of who we are. When we love ourselves, or another person, we fulfill the purpose of Creation and we feel the love of God, for all love comes from God. We are merely channels for divine love. When we love God for "no reason," not for what He will do for us, but for God alone, He fills us with a great love.

At the root of all the desires we may have for money, fame or meaningful relationships is the pure and simple desire of the soul to love and to be known. In order to love freely and purely, we must remove the obstacles that block us from being in touch with our true essence. This is not so simple. We have to break down the walls we have constructed to protect ourselves from being hurt by other people. We have to let go of our fears and allow ourselves to be open and vulnerable. Love asks us to transcend our ego and sense of separateness and self-importance, to become giving and expanded rather than selfish and limited. Kabbalah teaches that the main challenge we have in life is to transform the desire to receive for ourselves into the desire to share with others. This challenge confronts us daily in all our interactions with others. Am I going to open my heart and let the natural flow of love come through me or will I block it with self-absorbed concerns and fears?

How do we become more giving and less selfish? First, we recognize that we are all interconnected. We are taught through kabbalah that each person is part of a larger original soul that we call *Adam*. When we give to another person, we are in essence giving to ourselves. This is a most important concept. When we give, we are expanding our sense of self. Our life is broader and richer. When we are in touch with the divine within us and allow God's love to be expressed through us, we first receive this love and light ourselves. By giving to others, we essentially give to ourselves. It is a great joy to experience ourselves as givers. Rabbi Eliyahu Dessler, a twentieth-century leader in the Mussar movement, said in his book *Strive for Truth* that when we give to someone they become a part of us. We have a stake in their well-being. The more we give, the greater we become. Our lives are greater than our own. Our lives include many others as well. We have to realize that by giving we do not become less but more.

On the physical level, it would appear that when we give, we have less. Sometimes we are afraid that we will be diminished by giving. We are afraid that we will be taken advantage of, exploited or controlled by loving. However, on the spiritual level, we actually increase what we have and become greater. If we truly give to others for the sake of giving, for the pleasure of giving, then our giving is not a ruse for taking, as it often is. When we give without expectation, we are in no way obligating the other to give back to us. There is freedom and joy in such giving. When we give in this way, God's love flows through us. Giving is a spiritual discipline that requires commitment and effort. We constantly face opportunities to give or to restrain. It is a well-established spiritual principle that whatever we give for a *mitzvah,* God pays back with interest.

My teacher, Reb Shlomo Carlebach, used to walk the streets of New York, asking people if there was anything he could do for them. He collected a congregation of homeless people as his followers. On more than one occasion, they saved Shlomo's life and that of other Jews. One of these "miracle" stories occurred in Harlem when someone's car unexpectedly broke down on a deserted street. In a split second, a group of men appeared and began to threaten the traveler's life. One man who happened to pass by noticed the skullcap on the traveler's head, like the one that Reb Shlomo always wore, and asked, "Do you know Shlomo Carlebach?" The traveler replied, "Of course." Because of his connection to Reb Shlomo, the man told the others to let the traveler go, and they did.

In human relationships, particularly between men and women, love is often problematic. Though love is natural, it is not always easy to love. Sometimes it is not clear what love is. Within every person is a desire to love and be loved. Yet it is very difficult for people to get together these days. People tell us they love us one day, and on another day they tell us they do not. Is love just an ephemeral feeling? Does it last? How can we hold onto love? Under what conditions may love be lasting? *Ethics of the Fathers* (Pirkei

Avos), the book of ethical teachings of the sages of Israel, teaches us about the essence of love: "Love that is dependent upon a specific consideration . . . when that consideration vanishes, the love ceases. But if love is not dependent upon a specific consideration, it will never cease." Unconditional love is precious, holy and very rare. Unconditional love has no bottom line. It is an expression of our highest choice.

The best reason to love someone is "for no reason." We love because we have made a decision to love, and this decision is followed with the commitment and dedication to love. Unconditional love is eternal precisely because it is not based on anything. The Torah says that conditional love will always dissipate. Many times we love what is external to others. We love their appearance, we love their wit, their status; we love them because we feel good when we are near them, but do we really love them? Love based on external factors will not last. In the challenging situations of life, love is tested, and if people grow through that test, their love is refined and strengthened.

When I was in high school, I read a book that entered the depths of my heart. I recall it now as I write. In *The Art of Loving*, Erich Fromm stated that there are two types of love. The first is narcissistic love: "I love you because I need you." The other is mature love: "I need you because I love you." Narcissistic love is conditional because it is predicated on meeting your own needs and is about taking rather than giving: "I love you because you meet my needs." The implication is "When you stop meeting my needs or you challenge me too much, I will not love you and I will leave you, or I will find someone else who meets my needs better than you do, and I will leave you for that person." With such "love," people often live in fear that the love they have received will not last. These relationships are more about control and dependency than love.

Mature love, "I need you because I love you," is unconditional love. A person loving in a mature way recognizes that he has a need to love. This is nothing to be ashamed about. We need to love. It is actually our greatest need, after physical needs such as breathing, eating and sleeping. Loving brings purpose and meaning to our lives. Loving enables us to touch that deep reservoir of love within us, and it feels great! When we truly love someone, we are not afraid or ashamed of loving.

What is love? Why is it important to love? How can we become truly loving people? The search for love is actually the search for God. Through acts of love, we transcend our limited selves and reach for something sublime. Love enables us to go beyond our own self-interests. When we truly love, we feel God's presence within us, and this feels wonderful. We often think that when we love another person, that other person is the source of our love, but it actually is our own love we experience. It is our connection to God within us that enables us to love. We do not love because of what we will receive, but through love we receive the love we are giving. And this is more than enough. There is freedom and joy in true loving because we do not need people to be different from how they are. We love people as they are. When we love, we are in touch with God within ourselves, and we see God within others. God made people intrinsically and extremely lovable. When we truly love we do not see our beloveds as extensions of ourselves, but we see the essence of their souls.

Be grateful for the opportunities to love. Create opportunities to love within your life. Everyone becomes greater through love, even though we also become more vulnerable through love. Reb Shlomo Carlebach once said, "Love makes us whole and yet it breaks our hearts." Love takes us to the depths of our hearts. Perhaps it is the vulnerability that love awakens within us that makes love so precious, opening us up to God in greater intimacy. Love teaches us that it is safe and liberating to be vulnerable. Love brings deep joy and meaning, reverence and awe to life.

Rabbi Simon Jacobson said that the Torah teaches us how to love because through it we learn how to connect with something greater than ourselves. All of the Torah laws are designed to teach us how to transcend our personal impulses and connect directly with God, the source of all love. For example, we may like to eat certain foods, but we learn to restrain ourselves for a higher connection with God. We learn to put aside our work on the Sabbath even though we may need the money or enjoy our work. It is often asked, if this is true, why do we find many traditional Jews who are not loving? Rabbi Jacobson responds that these people keep the Torah on a rote level.

They follow the rules, but they are not open to the inner dimension, the spirit of the law. This is an important comment. People who are naturally loving would be even more loving by connecting to Torah. It provides a vast arena for channeling love.

Rabbi Eliyahu Dessler provided a great deal of clarity on the subject of love. He asked an interesting and important question in *Strive for Truth:* "Is giving the result of love or does love come from giving? Do we give to people we love? Or do we love people we give to?" It is customary to think that giving is a byproduct of love. We love someone so we give to him. This is true. But Reb Dessler said that if you want to love others, you should give to them. Become involved in something that is for their benefit. Giving breaks down the psychological barriers between people. We come to love the person we have given to or nurtured.

I am reminded of a beautiful story I read in high school entitled *The Little Prince* by Antoine de Saint-Exupéry. During one of his many travels to different planets, the Little Prince goes to a planet where he sees a garden of beautiful roses. At first this discovery proves disorienting to him because he had a rose on his own planet that he loved and cared for very much. He thought he loved his rose because she was unique and the most beautiful thing he ever saw. When he is confronted with so many roses as beautiful as his, he questions his love. Why did he think his rose was special? He then realizes that he loved his rose because he tended to her, he watered her, he weeded the area around her, which explains why the rose will always be precious to him. It is his rose. In the same way, we come naturally to love people we care for and give to. We have a stake in their well-being. The only reason that a person is a stranger, according to Reb Dessler, is that we have not yet given to him. If you bestow goodness on every single person you meet, you will feel close to everyone.

People who want to love look for opportunities to be loving. Abraham is our model for selfless love. He was constantly looking for people upon whom to bestow kindness. Giving hospitality to strangers is a great *mitzvah*. The Bible tells us quite often "to love the stranger." Religious people are most noted for opening their homes in this way. If you want to experience a *Shabbos* or a Jewish holiday celebration, it is not too difficult to obtain an invitation to a Jewish person's home. Most orthodox synagogues, and especially Lubavitch synagogues, will make an effort to secure such an invitation for you, especially if you have never had such an experience. Don't deprive yourself. Your hosts will be happy they had the opportunity to do this *mitzvah*.

Parenting is a challenging and transforming opportunity for people to learn about the depths of unconditional love. A healthy love between a parent and a child is the most natural love. A couple bears children mostly so they can bestow and express their united love. If they cannot have children, a couple will sometimes adopt. God made babies cute and adorable so that parents could not help but fall in love with them. Most people learn how to love more deeply as parents than they were capable of before they were parents. They learn how to demonstrate a selfless and unconditional love. It does not matter what the child does. Regardless of what children do, they will never lose their parents' love. The love of a parent for a child is such a strong love that the bond can never be severed.

Yet it is possible that many parents are not able to rise to this opportunity. There are parents who are neglectful and abusive. Yet the fifth commandment is "Honor your father and mother, so that you will live a long life." Many people wonder how they can honor a parent who has been abusive to them. It is interesting to note the Torah tells us to honor our parents "so that you will live a long life," but it does not command us to love them. Perhaps a person lives longer if by honoring his parents he can overcome the ways he feels limited or hurt. This commandment asks us to forgive our parents for the injustices they committed and to remember that, for whatever reason, these individuals were chosen to be the divine conduits for our birth. By honoring our parents, we honor God.

In healthy families, siblings feel a natural and unconditional love for each other. This is considered a steady love. You may divorce your spouse, but your sibling will always be your sibling. Though siblings may sometimes have to overcome jealousy, they learn how to share with others, which is very important. They have a history with each other that is special and lasts forever.

Marriage is the ultimate expression of God's love. The Talmud says that finding our soul mate, getting married, is like crossing the Red Sea. This is an allusion to the parting of the Red Sea, which allowed the Jewish people to cross that water as they fled from Egypt. What does this mean? On the simple level, everyone knows that getting married is like jumping into water. Marriage is an unknown. It doesn't matter how long you have known the person. You don't know what marriage is until you're married. On a deeper level, in comparing marriage to the Red Sea, the Talmud imparts an important teaching about love. It is the nature of the sea to be water, but the sea was willing to change its nature to become dry land because there was a need. The oral teachings of the *midrash* say that the water arose and formed twelve columns so that each of the twelve tribes had its own passageway. The Red Sea was able to be simultaneously wet and dry. In a similar vein, love asks us to be willing to change our nature, to withdraw and make space, to become one with another person, and also to remain an individual.

In a good marriage, there should also be an unconditional love between the spouses. This may be the hardest challenge and the greatest demonstration of unconditional love because marriages occur between people of different backgrounds who are not bonded by blood. Marriage is made even harder because people so often are attracted to and marry the very people who push their buttons the most. Marriages take much dedication and work to be successful. We are challenged to grow in love. To have a loving marriage, we have to let go of the ways in which we do not really love ourselves and of the protective barriers that separate us from the beloved. Love asks us to be in touch with and responsible for our feelings and communicate them to our beloved. Love asks us to listen and respect the feelings and thoughts of our beloveds even if they are different from ours or contrary to our self-interest. If we are open and worthy, love affords us an opportunity to be so much more than we thought we could be before. If we can love our spouses unconditionally, we will experience a oneness with them that parallels the closeness we can experience with God. When a couple unites their bodies, their minds and their souls, they know Godliness. This is the most fulfilling and most healing love.

Loving is a spiritual discipline that can take us to the greatest heights. It is a spiritual path that expands with each step. We begin by loving ourselves and receiving the love that God and our families have for each of us. In the kabbalistic practice of assigning numerical values to the Hebrew letters, connection is made between words that have the same numerical value. The Hebrew word for love, *ahavah*, and the Hebrew word for one, *echod*, add up to thirteen. This equates to "Love brings oneness." This also reminds us of the thirteen attributes of God's compassion revealed to Moses when he received forgiveness for the Jewish people's creation of the golden calf, and it teaches us that to love we need to be forgiving and compassionate.

As we grow in our capacity to love, our circle of love expands to include friends and teachers. We allow more and more people to enter the innermost realms of our being. In his book *The Moral Principles,* Rabbi Abraham Isaac Kook, the first chief rabbi of the Yishuv, the Zionist settlement and community that preceded the State of Israel, tells us that we should love all people, love all nations, and desire their spiritual and material advancement. Though our love for people must be all-inclusive, embracing wicked people as well, it does not mean that we do not hate evil itself. We are to hate evil but love the wicked person because of the good within him and because he was created by God. Loving all people takes discipline and effort for most people. According to Rav Kook, loving the Jewish people includes loving all people because the Jewish people are destined to serve toward the perfection of all things.

The Jewish people are a very diverse group. As the saying goes, with two Jews there are three synagogues: The synagogue each one goes to and the synagogue neither would go to. The politics in Jewish life are divisive and repelling. Yet the greater collective soul of the Jewish people is easy to love. We just need to tap into it. We do not have to create this love. It is there for us if we are open to it. It is our heritage. The Jewish people are an extended though at times dysfunctional family, but a family nevertheless. There are many Jews who have risen to the opportunity of loving the Jewish people, each Jew unconditionally. These are righteous and holy people, and they bind Jews together. They are called "the foundation." And among the Jewish people are especially loving souls who love everything and everyone that God created as if they were parts of themselves.

This is an even higher demonstration of love.

I am reminded of some stories that testify how love, even if it is unrequited, may take us to the greatest spiritual heights. The first story is from the *Reishit Chochma,* a classical kabbalistic book of ethics and moral perfection. In one story, a poor man falls deeply in love with a very beautiful princess. He builds up his courage and asks to court her. Shocked that a commoner would approach her, she spurns him sharply and says, "I'll see you in the graveyard." By this she means that she will have nothing to do with him while she is alive, but she acknowledges that as human beings they will be equal in death.

He, however, responds to her words literally. He goes to the cemetery and waits for her. Time passes and his yearning for her increases. He speaks continually of his love for her. He is afraid to leave the cemetery because she might come and he would miss her. People have compassion on him and bring him food. With the passage of time, his anticipation increases. His longing intensifies with each day. He welcomes each new day as it will bring him closer to his beloved. Because of his love, he never doubts that she will come. His concentration on her becomes more and more focused. He meditates on nothing but her, and his love for her purifies him. He is immersed in his love for the beloved.

This love is the doorway to a higher love. It elevates him until he transcends materiality. He transcends his physical body and time. He comes to love and merge with the source of all love, the *Shechinah,* the Divine Presence. Within his one-pointed focus, he is often in intoxicated states of consciousness. People start to come to him for blessings. When word gets out that his blessings have power, many more people gather around him. Though they bestow much honor upon him, he is oblivious to it. He is lovesick for the *Shechinah.*

Many years ago I heard a similar and beautiful Hindu story. It is also a powerful example of the depths of love. Because I don't remember any of the actual names, I will give all the characters Hebrew names. The message of this story is very Jewish to me. A man—we will call him Yehuda—falls in love with a princess, the king's daughter, who we will call Yekera Kadisha, which means "holy and precious." Yehuda is constantly reciting her name: "Yekera Kadisha." He enters into states of bliss thinking of her, chanting her name and yearning for her. He can do nothing else. The king has compassion on him and proclaims that the people of the kingdom should feed and care for Yehuda who calls out the name of the king's daughter wherever he roams.

Soon dozens of men claim to be Yehuda, calling out "Yekera Kadisha." Not being able to distinguish who is the real Yehuda, the people feed all the men. The number of Yehudas in the kingdom increases with each day. They all continuously call out with great love and yearning the name of the king's daughter. They all enter states of intoxication, and they are all fed by the people of the kingdom.

Upon hearing of this situation, the king becomes aware that these men are taking advantage of his goodness. He then issues a decree that anyone calling out the name of his daughter will be killed. All of a sudden there is only one Yehuda calling out the name. He is the one who truly loves the princess. All the others were just impostors who faked love because of the material benefits they received. The real Yehuda loves the princess, not because of what he receives from her, but simply because he loves her.

The story has a happy ending for the power of real love is very great. Because Yehuda loves the princess so truly, she begins to feel love for him. Yekera Kadisha begins to wander through the palace crying out, "Yehuda, Yehuda, Yehuda!" The king tries to distract her, but whenever he suggests something, all the princess can say is, "Will Yehuda be there?" The king realizes that these lovers should be together. Because of his great love, Yehuda attains Yekera Kadisha. The moral of the story is that true love is irresistible to people and also to God.

11

THE KABBALAH OF SEXUALITY

We live in a time of increasing openness about sexuality, and as a culture we are preoccupied and obsessed with sex. Sex is talked about very casually on television and in newspapers in a way that did not even occur twenty years ago, during the time of the so-called "sexual revolution." In spite of all this openness, sexual relations in the modern world are still problematic. It appears that there is more sexual expression but less love—and less joy. In our fast-paced, consumer-oriented society, we are quickly losing the art of intimacy, the capacity to be with ourselves and with one another in a totally honest and respectful way. Judaism has much wisdom to offer about sexual relations, which I believe you will find interesting, helpful and elevating.

Judaism is the only ancient religion that affirms marriage and sexual relations bring a person to a higher state of holiness than abstinence. Jewish sages and prophets all married and bore children. According to many Jewish sages, when done at the proper time with the proper intention, sex is the highest and holiest experience available to human beings. According to the Ramban (Nachmanides), sex brings wholeness not only to ourselves, but it also radiates spiritual energy and healing to the world. Many other spiritual traditions teach that a person who aspires to levels of holiness and heightened spiritual awareness must be celibate and generally separate from the physical world to be more fully immersed in Godliness. Judaism is different. Judaism is about being in your body, in your life in this physical world in a holy way. We have a soul and we have a body. In truth, we are in this physical world as physical beings for just a brief period of time. We will have much time to be in the spiritual world when we are not in a physical body.

In some other spiritual or religious traditions, there is a division between the physical and the spiritual aspects of life. God is viewed as spiritual, so if people want to be close to God, they must separate themselves from the physical aspects of life to immerse themselves in spirituality. They will abstain or have sex as infrequently as possible. Judaism has a totally different perspective. God is not spiritual, and God is not physical. Physicality and spirituality are both creations of God. God encompasses and unifies them. God is within the physical, and God is within the spiritual. When we make unifications between the physical and the spiritual, we glimpse the underlying Godliness.

Judaism is all about unification. Every holy act is done for the purpose of uniting God with the Divine Presence, the *Shechinah*. For example, Jews say blessings before and after eating to sanctify the mundane physical act of eating. Because our sexuality is such a powerful biological and physical urge, and because it also connects us to the deepest and innermost core of our souls, it provides us with the opportunity to make the highest forms of unification. There is great joy when all parts of our being can be united in a single act in the experience of becoming one with another person. The Bible tells us, "Man should leave his father and mother and cling to his wife and become one flesh" (Gen. 2:24). This is what God wants. The sexual act is brief, but its effects spill over to all aspects of our life.

Sex, which has the potential to take us to the heights of human experience, can also take us to the lowest depths. Judaism says that sex without connection to love or God is an animalistic act. There is no real intimacy or healing possible in such an act. Even from some of my male therapy clients, I hear that such sex is unsatisfying and meaningless to them. The Ramban states that if our sexuality is expressed just to meet our physical desires, the Divine Presence leaves us. Furthermore, purely lustful sex, even between consenting adults, is negative and harmful. It undermines whatever spirituality is present and creates *klippot,* opaque shells, which shut out the Light of the Divine Presence. Sexual activity of this nature leaves its traces on the human soul. Whenever you are physically intimate with another person, you are connected to that person forever. An authentic kabbalist will easily detect whether a person has had many sexual partners and whether the unions were lustful.

Many people attempt to meet their needs for emotional intimacy through sexual relations. We all have a need to be held, caressed and loved. These are real needs that should be honored. However, it is best that people meet those needs directly instead of confusing them with sexuality. Some people deceive themselves by saying that they can have a casual sexual relationship with no strings attached, only to find that they are ultimately hurt in such a venture. Sex is never neutral. It is a distortion of the holiness of sex to use sexual relations to meet our emotional needs. There is no reason to have sexual relations if your real need is to be hugged.

According to the Bible, the first human, Adam, was androgynous. Adam was both male and female. Then God said, "It is not good for man to be alone" (Gen. 2:18). Taking flesh and bone from the side of Adam, God then formed two separate beings, man and woman, who stood opposite each other. This separation into man and woman left each looking for the being they had been. This is the basis for sexual attraction, the sexual drive and passion men and women experience toward the other. It is the drive for unification, for wholeness. The *Zohar* says that no male or female soul can be a complete human soul without the other.

A couple should be aware that by having sexual relations they are fulfilling God's Will and that the pleasure they experience also comes from God. When God created everything He said, "And it was good." When He created man, God said, "It is very good" (Gen. 1:31). Bible commentators say that "very good" refers to the two inclinations that man was given, the *yetzer tov,* the good inclination, and the *yetzer hara,* the evil inclination. In proper sexual relations, these two inclinations are united. Without the *yetzer hara,* we would have no passion or sexual desire. When the *yetzer hara* is united with the *yetzer tov* for Godliness, as in sexual relations, it is "very good."

Yet even deeper in the soul at the heart of sexual desire is the longing to unite with God and to know Him in a very direct way. The sexual desire is actually a spiritual desire to transcend the physical body, to let go of our boundaries and merge with God. This sexual drive is a gift from God that He implanted within us. When done in the proper way with the proper intention, sex, according to Judaism, is actually an essential spiritual practice that allows us to enter into the highest realms of holiness. It is not holy because it perpetuates the species, though it does this because it is holy. It is holy because, through our sexuality, we touch and open to the innermost places in our being and that of our beloved. In the sexual act, we may be naked and not ashamed.

The Ramban told us that when the Bible says "Adam knew his wife," this refers to the act of sexual relations. He elaborated on the word "knowing" by saying that sperm actually come from the brain of the man. Therefore, intention is most important. Sexuality should embrace and unite all parts of ourselves in a single act. For our sexuality to be a "knowing" experience, it must engage us physically, emotionally, intellectually and spiritually. Through the act of sexuality we may know ourselves and another in the most holy and elevated way. There is no shame or guilt in such sex, only the awareness of beauty, preciousness and holiness. This divine gift fills us with a deep sense of gratitude for being alive in a physical body. It must be treasured and respected.

To prepare for the holiness of sexual relations, the couple is advised to do a *mitzvah* prior to sexual intercourse, such as study Torah, say Psalms or give to charity. Some religious men wash their hands in the same ritual way as if they were preparing to eat bread or bestow the priestly blessing. This kind of hand washing is not about personal hygiene but about purification of intention, the necessary preparation before engaging in an act of holiness. Just as we have the intention before prayer, meditation and learning Torah to unify the Holy One, Blessed Be He, with the *Shechinah,* so, similarly, a couple should have this intention before sexual intercourse.

Intention is most important. Having sexual relations is a *mitzvah* like any other. We may make the most direct connection to Godliness through sex.

Jewish sages, such as the Ramban, have given detailed instructions on how to engage in sexual relations. Prior to sexual intercourse, a couple must have the intention to come close to each other and to God through this act. In Judaism, the home is considered to be a miniature Holy Temple, and the bedroom is called the "Holy of Holies." The bedroom is symbolic of the holiest place in the Temple where the high priest pronounced the name of God and atoned for the people. In Jewish practice, God is invited into the bedroom. Each partner should behold the Godliness of the other. Some sages even suggested that each behold the other as an incarnation of God. The woman should be honored by her husband as the Divine Presence Herself and she should behold her husband as the Holy One.

Before and during sexual relations, the rabbis advise a man to speak lovingly to his beloved, to be gentle, to make her happy and to focus more on her sexual arousal than on his own. Since it is actually a *mitzvah* for a man to satisfy his wife, he should do whatever he can to bring his wife to orgasm before he has one. Foreplay is encouraged. Kissing before and during the sexual act is important. The *Zohar* says that kissing brings the greatest union of spirit. Kissing awakens the desire and love of cleaving. The *Zohar* likens the lips to wings that raise a person higher and higher. This is why the *Song of Songs,* written by King Solomon, uses erotic metaphors to speak of the love between the soul and God, between the Jewish people and God. It begins with "Let Him kiss me with the kisses of His mouth, for His love is sweeter than wine."

Sexual relations are holy because we procreate through them. This is actually the first commandment that God gave to people. "Be fruitful and multiply." God chose to perpetuate the species by us having sexual relations. He could have done it differently. We did not necessarily have to be involved. It could have happened in another way. Yet God gave us the gift of participating in Creation with Him. Using sexual relations as the vehicle for the perpetuation of the species, God involves us in the deepest, most intimate way. For better or worse, God made man and woman attracted to each other and also dependent on each other. They cannot have a child by themselves, at least not yet. Even with all our modern technology, we still need an egg and we still need a sperm.

The Gemara says that there are three partners in the creation of a child: the father, the mother and God. Kabbalah comments that the father's seed creates everything in the body that is white, such as the brain, the nails, the white of the eyes, the teeth, the intestines. The woman produces everything that is red, such as the blood, skin, heart, liver, gallbladder, dark part of the eyes. God creates the soul. Yet the couple's intention and consciousness at the time of conception determine the kind of soul they will attract to them. Souls are said to hover around the bed at the time of sexual relations. If the couple is ruled by lust at that time, they generally attract a less spiritually refined soul to birth. If the couple have the intention to have sexual relations as a spiritual practice, they will attract a more spiritual, easy-tempered soul. According to kabbalah, if a man woos his woman with sweet words, kissing and foreplay and the woman has an orgasm first, the couple will have a male child. It goes without saying that a man may not force himself sexually on his wife or any other woman.

Judaism recommends that the best day to have sexual relations is *Shabbos,* the holiest day of the week. Unlike other traditions that refrain from sexual relations on holy days, Jews are encouraged to have sex particularly on holy days. Having sex is actually a *mitzvah*. Having sex at other times is fine, but having sexual relations adds extra joy and festivity to *Shabbos* and holidays. *Shabbos* is celebrated with prayers, singing and festive meals, and sexual relations for the couple is the pinnacle of the *Shabbos* celebrations. As the Divine Presence is felt more on *Shabbos* and holidays, there is more energy to be used in sexual relations. Also, people are freed from the pressures of work. It is said, too, that on *Shabbos* a person has an extra soul, which means that a person has increased spiritual receptivity and capacity.

The Ramban advised a couple to wait, however, until food is digested. Sex should not occur immediately after eating. Fertility is reduced at this time. If a child is conceived during this time, the child will have spiritual handicaps that will take a lifetime to correct. A couple should wait to have sexual relations until their bodies are not hungry, not full and not weak.

It is best that the man be even-tempered during sexual relations. Then the soul that will be attracted to the couple will also be balanced and even-tempered. If the man is too passionate or even angry at the time of sexual relations, the child will also be angry and easily agitated. The best time is during the second half of the night, right after midnight. According to kabbalah, the gates of compassion open at midnight. This is considered the best time to give birth to holy seed.

Thousands of years before Masters and Johnson researched human sexuality, Judaism recognized not only that women have sexual needs but that their capacity for sexual pleasure is even greater than that of men. Sexual relations were traditionally a woman's entitlement. The Talmud specifies that a man has an obligation to have sexual relations with his wife and to satisfy her sexually. According to Jewish law, a married woman is entitled to food, clothing, shelter and sexual relations. A husband cannot diminish his wife's sexual pleasure. For example, he should not take business trips making himself unavailable to fulfill his marital duty of sexual relations at times when his wife is available. He cannot say that he is too holy to have sexual relations unless she agrees with him. The woman in a marriage determines the time and frequency of sexual relations.

According to Jewish law, sexual relations are not allowed during a woman's menstrual period and for a number of days after that. At the appropriate time, women go to the *mikvah*, the ritual bath, for immersion. After that, sexual relations may resume. I know that many women are uncomfortable with this ancient ritual of *mikvah*. They think that it infers that women are unclean. I would wager that most of the women who object to *mikvah* have not experienced it themselves. Nor do they understand its spiritual significance. Most women who take on the *mitzvah* of going to the *mikvah* love it. It is a time for a woman to be free of the responsibilities of child rearing, to be with herself in a nurturing way, to take a luxurious bath, to meditate and to know that by doing these nurturing acts she is fulfilling God's law. The *mikvah* itself is a very powerful and wonderful spiritual experience, imparting a feeling of holiness. It is actually an honor and a privilege to be commanded to go to *mikvah*.

The Rambam said, "If a person immerses himself in the *mikvah* with the intention of becoming pure, he is pure." "Impurity" in Hebrew, *tameh,* means "to be closed," cut off from the life force. "Purification" in Hebrew, *tahor,* makes you open. It is interesting that the Hebrew word for "hope" is *tikvah,* very similar to *mikvah.* It is said that *mikvah* restores hope in a person. Being totally immersed in water puts you in touch instantly with the depths of your own soul, with what you really want in your life. In the *mikvah* you feel that you have returned to the womb and are immersed in Godliness. This is said to be the most auspicious time to ask for anything you want.

I hope that each of you, men and women alike, avail yourselves of this experience at least once in your lives. If you decide to go to the *mikvah,* prior to going you might want to read *Waters of Eden* by Aryeh Kaplan. It is good to meditate before the actual immersion, to go deep inside to connect with the desire within you to be purified. If you feel guilty about something, you can pray that immersing in the *mikvah* will help remove the residue of impurity that remains attached to you. If you want to be more spiritually open, to be filled with greater joy and love to do what you need to do in your life, pray for that as well. In the *mikvah,* I feel a sense of awe and a deep bonding with the Jewish people, particularly women. *Mikvah* is an ancient practice and a most important ritual connecting us to the Jewish lineage in a visceral way. According to Jewish law, if a community has limited resources, it is more important to build a *mikvah* than to build a synagogue.

While anyone, even non-Jews, can go to the *mikvah* for spiritual uplifting or cleansing, a woman is obligated according to Jewish law to go to the *mikvah* following menstruation and before resuming sexual relations with her husband. At the time of immersion, the woman says a blessing to align herself with the Divine Will and the sexual relations that will take place. It is good for a man to go to the *mikvah* as well, but he is not commanded to do so and has no blessing to say. A woman who goes to the *mikvah* is less likely to be seen as a sex object.

Her husband respects her and senses the *Shechinah* around her. Most importantly, she senses this about herself.

Certain laws safeguard the holiness of sexual relations in Judaism. Accordingly, there are times each month that couples refrain from sexual relations and times when they can immerse themselves as much as they want. Many say that this keeps sexual passion alive in a marriage while also providing time for a couple to focus respectfully on their friendship and differentiation.

Though Judaism affirms that sexual relations are best expressed in the context of marriage, there is another category in Jewish law called *pelaigish,* "concubine," which allows for sexual relations that occur outside the context of marriage. The couple have an understanding between the two of them, and the woman goes to the *mikvah* as if she were married. This was discussed in the Talmud thousands of years ago, before it was a common practice for people to live together before marriage, and in some religious circles it was considered an acceptable option. Sometimes a couple would choose not to marry for a number of reasons, a practice that occurs now with greater frequency.

PART THREE

THE NEW AGE IS <u>SO</u> JEWISH

12

DO JEWS BELIEVE IN ANGELS?

Angels have become mainstream in the New Age. Quite a few books containing accounts of persons being rescued by angels are being published and selling very well. A popular television show features angels as the main characters. But the phenomenon of encounters with angels is not new. The Bible contains many references to angels. Abraham was visited by three angels after he circumcised himself. One angel comforted him, another told him about the planned destruction of Sodom and Gomorrah, and the third told him that he and Sarah would give birth to a son. Many other contacts with angels have been recorded. Hagar was comforted by an angel. Jacob saw angels "running and returning" up a ladder. Chana was told by an angel that she would give birth to a son. An angel, a seraph, touched Isaiah on his mouth before he received prophecy.

In my own family's oral history my grandfather and grandmother recalled two encounters with angels that were passed down to me. In one incident in eastern Europe, my grandfather was helping his father carry wood in a wagon. Late one Friday afternoon on their way home, they had to climb a steep hill with a very tired horse. At the foot of this hill leading to their home, they put their shoulders to the wagon to help the horse. The wagon moved slowly, but soon there was difficulty. The horse could not get the wagon to budge; it even seemed to be slipping backward.

They continued their efforts with no success. It was late, and as an orthodox Jew my grandfather needed to be home before *Shabbos*. The horse kept straining and they kept pushing to no avail. Suddenly a tall, muscular peasant appeared, put his shoulder to the wagon and easily pushed it to the top of the hill. He then vanished into the trees at the side of the road. My grandfather, a young boy at the time, looked at his father and said, "I don't understand." He was told, "Shush, no questions. It was a *malach* (an angel)." Whether this was a true encounter with an angel we cannot know for sure. However, what is more interesting is that the kindness of a stranger could be attributed to an angel. This shows that the possibility of such an encounter was very much part of the culture of the religious Jews at that time.

The belief in angels is integral to traditional Jewish spiritual and religious practice. Every *Shabbos* most Jews greet the angels with a special song. We invoke them, we ask them to bless us and then we send them on their way. Three times a day, in traditional prayer services, the highest point of the service is when we chant the very words that are attributed to the angels. We stand with our feet together to imitate the stance of angels and we chant, "Holy, Holy, Holy, the whole world is filled with His glory." By imitating the position and the chanting, we hope to experience the consciousness of the angels, who were created to praise God. In the traditional prayer books, like *Art Scroll* and *Tehilat Hashem* (Lubavitch), is a prayer to be recited at bedtime that asks for the protection of the archangels Michael, Gabriel, Uriel and Raphael. When I mentioned this in one of my classes, one student was very surprised. She thought that these angels were Christian. While Christianity may have placed more emphasis on angels, the knowledge of angels comes from Judaism.

According to kabbalah, hundreds and thousands of angels are all around us. They are not usually visible to us, because they are not physical in the way that we are. According to the Bible, most angels were created primarily on the fifth day of Creation, before the creation of man, which occurred on the sixth day. Angels are made out of the elements of fire and air. We human beings consist of four elements: fire, water, air and earth. Angels can see us, but we cannot see or hear angels unless they make it possible. Many kinds of angels reside in each of the spiritual worlds, which are not in heaven or a faraway galaxy. Rather, our physical world is contained within the spiritual worlds. Perhaps it is best to liken the spiritual world to a reality of another dimension, another vibration within our reality. Take comfort that we are surrounded by angels.

Many angels have names because they have permanent existence, such as the highest angels, the archangels Michael, Gabriel, Uriel, Raphael and Metratron. Though these angels reside in the highest spiritual worlds, they interact with our physical world. Every time my meditation students and I sing a *niggun* composed by Reb Shlomo Carlebach to the words of the bedtime prayer service and intended to invoke the archangels, we are amazingly enrobed in the most loving energy.

Many other angels are nameless and short-lived. Some angels, such as the seraphim, who are continually burning up as they come close to God, reside in the higher spiritual worlds. Other angels, such as the *chayot,* travel between the spiritual worlds. In Ezekiel's vision, the *chayot* were "running and returning like a vision of lightning." The function of angels is to "run and return," to constantly be the messengers for the flow of Divine Light through the worlds.

Other angels facilitate the interaction between the physical world and the spiritual worlds, such as the *ophanim,* also called "wheels" in reference to what Ezekiel saw in his prophecy. Like wheels, the *ophanim* constantly raise the physical up to the spiritual and bring spiritual illumination to the physical. Other spiritual entities are like angels, but they are demons, *shedim.* They also have particular functions and limitations and cause the evil in the world.

The spiritual and the physical worlds are interconnected. According to the Jewish tradition, everything that occurs in our world, every process, every event takes place under the charge of some type of angel, with the exception of childbirth, rain and resurrection, which remain under God's direct care, according to the *Zohar.* The Talmud says that even a blade of grass does not grow unless an angel tells it to grow.

It is also true that the upper world acts upon impulses sent from below. It is not just our actions but also our words and our thoughts that impact the spiritual forces. Our thoughts are probably the most potent agent we have, which is why true concentrated prayer and meditation are so beneficial. We can change reality with our thoughts and our prayers. Heartfelt prayer ascends directly to the spiritual worlds, which in turn creates a response from above. If a person does not pray with heart, it is possible that the prayer does not go up. Particular angels await our prayers. The *Zohar,* commenting on the Torah portion of Lech Lecha, says that 128,000 winged creatures flit around the world, ready to catch any voice they hear, good or bad, and to bring it up to heaven for judgment. In his commentary on *Sefer Yetzirah,* Rabbi Aryeh Kaplan said that stars are the standing points for angels. Divine Providence flows first through the angels, who in turn channel this influx through the stars and planets. Certain angels are associated with specific planets and astrological signs.

Angels are called *malachim,* which means "messengers." We do not pray to angels, for angels only carry out the will and orders of God. Rashi said it succinctly: "Angels carry prayers. Don't pray to angels." Some prayers are answered more quickly because they are offered with greater and purer *kavanna,* intention. If prayers are not answered, often we must work on purification. It may be dangerous for us to call on angels. If we do not purify ourselves properly, we could call upon a force that we do not know how to control, and this could be destructive. The names of angels are included in many prayer books; we are told to read their names but not to say them out loud. To say an angel's name out loud summons the angel.

If you call a certain angel, he comes down and then you realize you do not really need the angel, you still have to give that angel a message since you called him. The angel has to do something. If a destructive angel comes, you will have to tell him to destroy something that is in front of you or near you so he doesn't harm you. It is therefore best, and safer, for people to connect with God directly, rather than with the angels. God will send the proper angels.

When you pray, the angels take your prayers and bring them to God. The level of your soul and what you are asking for will determine the particular angel who will deliver your prayers. In the Gemara, Reb Yehuda said a person should not ask for his needs in Aramaic (which was the common language at the time of the writing of the Gemara). Angels do not understand Aramaic. Angels understand Hebrew. Therefore, it is important to pray for your needs in Hebrew. However, a sick person should use his own language because the *Shechinah,* the Divine Presence, is with a sick person, and the Divine Presence understands all languages. The language of tears is universal and is heard and responded to in heaven.

Though angels are not physical, they can assume a physical appearance as they did with Abraham in the Bible. Sometimes angels will reveal themselves to people to help them. Judaism also teaches that guardian angels are the souls of people who died but who do not want to reincarnate. Guardian souls, or angels, hover around people, guiding and protecting them from birth onward. We may also attract additional souls to help us through various experiences we have to go through in our lives.

Human beings have the potential to rise even higher than angels. At the *Shabbos* meal on Friday night, we call the angels to come to us and to bless us, and then we tell them to depart and bless others. Reb Eli Chaim Carlebach, Reb Shlomo's twin brother, once explained that after we receive the blessing of the angels we tell them to depart because we no longer need them. Once we are blessed, we are potentially higher and closer to God than angels.

The *midrash* says that the angels complained when God created man because God told the angels man would be higher than them. God took the birds and the animals and asked the angels to name each creature. The angels could not do so. God then took the same creatures and asked Adam to name them. Adam was able to give each one its correct name. According to kabbalah, letters contain the essential energies of all things, and thus combinations of letters—the names of things—contain the essential energies of those things. Adam was able to perceive the essence of every animal and bird and therefore state its correct name.

Human beings are considered unique in all Creation because we have been given the gift and the burden of free will. This is one reason why we have the possibility to be even higher than angels.

Our actions influence not only ourselves but also others in very direct ways. With our free will, we have the potential to influence God or reality. Humans are the only creatures with this ability. Angels and animals do not have free will or the ability to influence God and each other in the way that we do. However, our power to influence spiritual forces and the manner in which these forces will intervene in our world and change reality are still circumscribed by God.

We human beings are not just recipients of angelic or spiritual forces. We create angels and influence the spiritual forces. Our good deeds create good angels who protect us. Our bad deeds evoke persecuting angels who create challenge and difficulty for us. According to the *Zohar* and the Torah portion of Lech Lecha, the persecuting angels are most active between sundown and midnight. At midnight, the gates of compassion open.

According to a section in *Gates of Holiness* by Rabbi Hayim Vital, "We create angels by everything that we do—good and bad angels, according to the actions of the person. If the intention to study Torah is very pure, the angels which are created from this are very holy. If a person does a *mitzvah* like he is supposed to do, he creates a very holy angel. If the *mitzvah* is not complete, the angel created is missing part of its light."

Angels who reveal the future or tell secrets are called *maggidim*. There are human beings who have a *maggid,* but the *maggid* does not reveal itself to the person. Whether the *maggid* reveals itself depends on the soul and actions of the person. Rabbi Yosef Caro, who codified the *Shulchan Orach,* had a *maggid* and even wrote a book about it. There were many others, for example, Rabbi Moses Luzzatto, who wrote great philosophical works such as *Way of God* and *The Knowing Heart,* also had *maggidim*. If a person is made holy by learning Torah and doing *mitzvot,* the *maggid* he has will also be holy. There are also false *maggidim* who tell a mixture of lies. Because the person has a bad aspect in his character, so the angel he created is a mixture of good and bad. The *maggidim* come from each of the spiritual worlds.

Angels speak in a natural voice. Rabbi Vital goes on to say, "The secrets of prophecy come as a voice sent from above to speak with the prophet or the person who has the holy spirit. The voice cannot become real and enter into the ears of the prophet unless the voice is enrobed in the natural voice." This is the secret of the passage in Samuel that says, "The spirit of God spoke within me and His words are on my tongue." Samuel's prophecy came out as a voice. Angels speak as a voice with words and breath. The angels may also speak to a person in the breath or voice of a *tzaddik*. However, this cannot happen unless the recipient shares the same soul root (see chapter 13) with the *tzaddik*. If a person does a *mitzvah* according to the criteria of a particular *tzaddik,* that *tzaddik* may speak to him.

However, the Rambam (Maimonides), who we must understand was a rationalist, articulated a minority opinion regarding the existence of angels. The Rambam said that angels are not like physical beings but rather are "forces." For example, Rashi, the main Bible commentator, said that when Jacob wrestled with an angel he was wrestling with the angel of his brother Esau, but the Rambam commented that Jacob was actually wrestling with a part of his own soul.

According to the Rambam, angels are products of the imagination, but this does not make them false. Truth and reality are different. The prophet sees something that does not have objective reality, yet it is true according to his perceptions. According to the Rambam, people experience angels according to their preferences and abilities, but angels do not embody objective reality. For example, people may see angels with wings, but angels are not physical beings with wings. Rather, they are spiritual forces that are conceptualized and translated into images.

However, the Rambam did not believe that the idea of angels should be dismissed, because they can serve as very helpful symbols for expressing a person's potential, and he actually believed the idea should be cultivated. The Rambam's position in regard to angels remains controversial and is not generally accepted. Jewish tradition strongly favors the position of the Ramban (Nachmanides), who believed that angels do have objective reality.

13

REINCARNATION

Reincarnation is a popular topic of exploration in the emerging New Age. Reincarnation is also an ancient belief in many great spiritual traditions, but it has generally been closeted from the masses. Many people are surprised to discover that reincarnation is a belief in Judaism. Reb Shlomo Carlebach once said that in this lifetime we meet and become close to people we knew from previous lifetimes. He said that he did not have time to be with anyone he did not know before. This is true for all of us. According to kabbalah, most of the people with whom we are intimate, particularly kin such as our parents, siblings, children and spouses, are people we knew in other lifetimes.

Kabbalists trace throughout history the souls of many people reported in the Bible. For example, Abel, who died at the hand of Cain, was reincarnated as Moses, the greatest Jewish prophet. Some kabbalists say that Moses appeared later as Rabbi Simeon Bar Yochai, author of the *Zohar,* and again as Rabbi Yitzchok Luria, the great Safed kabbalist of the sixteenth century, and once again as the Baal Shem Tov, the founder in the eighteenth century of the Chassidic movement. According to the Arizel, Rabbi Akiva was a reincarnation of Korach, a leader of the rebellion against Moses in the desert, and then was reincarnated as his pupil Hayim Vital. The great rebbes of the past claimed to have had the power to read the past reincarnations of a person's soul.

The Jewish view of reincarnation is somewhat more elaborate and complex than Hindu or Buddhist perspectives. While the Buddhist and Hindu views state that the soul reincarnates as the same person in a new body, the Jewish perspective claims that this sometimes happens but mostly it is not so. According to Judaism, the soul consists of five levels: *nefesh, ruach, neshama, chaya* and *yehida* (see chapter 4). When the soul reincarnates, it most likely will not be the soul entirely as it was before. Only the levels of the soul that need fixing have to reincarnate. Generally, one does not obtain the same precious self in its entirety again. A reincarnated soul usually contains sparks or parts of another soul—or even a number of souls— that need to return to correct deficiencies or to ascend through the tests of human life. Each soul is a new and unique entity. The community of Israel is said to be made of 600,000 main souls, but there are more than 600,000 Jews in the world. How is this explained? Some souls share the same soul root.

Interestingly enough, a great soul usually reincarnates not in a single body but in many people. This increases the likelihood of the soul accomplishing its mission in this lifetime. In such cases, a number of people contain sparks from the very same soul. It would make sense that these people have a strong affinity for each other. Even though each soul is unique, people are part of soul groups or families, sharing sparks from the same great soul, the same soul root. We are affected by the actions of people in our soul group. Rabbi Yitzchok Luria said that sometimes a person may feel sad for no apparent reason; however, that is likely the result of a member of the soul family having a loss and everyone in that soul group being affected whether or not they personally know the person. It is also said that all Jews share a larger collective soul. Individual Jews, therefore, are uplifted and pained by the actions of the collective group. Our destinies are intertwined with each other.

Though the study of reincarnation is not "mainstream" Judaism, the Lubavitcher Rebbe recommended after the Holocaust that people know about reincarnation. Reincarnation provides a much needed perspective to understanding suffering. I have heard that both the Satmar Rebbe and the Lubavitcher Rebbe said that most of the Jewish souls born after World War II had undergone the Holocaust. I sense that this is true for me. When I was a very young child, I was obsessed with the Holocaust. Perhaps many of you were as well. At the ages of four and five, I was aware of the Holocaust and asked everyone I met why God allowed it to happen. As a child, I had frequent dreams of me running and running and running while trying to escape the Nazis. When I was in college I wrote a major paper trying to explain philosophically and religiously the suffering of the Holocaust. I often tell myself that whatever suffering I experience now is minute to the suffering that the Jewish people endured during the Holocaust.

Most suffering is considered an atonement for sins of another lifetime. There are many Chassidic stories illustrating this concept. One story is told of a man who came to the Alter Rebbe, Rabbi Schneur Zalman, founder of the Lubavitch Chassidic movement, requesting permission to divorce his wife. The man was very learned in Torah. Not only was his wife not interested in Torah learning, but she mocked his involvement. She taunted and humiliated him. Shouldn't he divorce her? The rebbe told the man to stay married to this woman even though she made his life difficult. The rebbe explained this advice on the basis of reincarnation. At the time of the First Temple, he said, this man was involved in idol worship. The rebbe said, "As atonement for this sin, you are married to this woman. God, so to speak, suffered humiliation by your involvement in idol worship, so similarly now you have to suffer humiliation from your wife."

The Hebrew word for "reincarnation" is *gilgul*. Gilgul means "wheel" or "rolling." The numerical value of the letters of this word is seventy-two. This is the same numerical value of the word *hesed*, lovingkindness. Reincarnation is considered *hesed* because it allows the soul to rectify its previous mistakes so that when it returns to the spiritual world it will be better able to absorb Godliness. If the soul doesn't correct its mistakes, returning to the physical world would once again be necessary. Returning to the physical world is a gamble for the soul. We have to be particularly careful with our intimate relationships, where the potential to hurt is the greatest. Assume that the people with whom we are intimate now are people we knew in other lifetimes. Most likely these relationships will challenge us in the very ways in which we have returned to fix and heal them. It will be helpful to keep this broader perspective in mind.

According to the *Zohar,* the Torah portion of Mishpatim is all about the secrets of reincarnation. The Torah describes the laws regarding slavery, yet the *Zohar* states that slavery refers to the laws regarding the transmigration of souls. Being in the physical body is equated with slavery. The Torah portion starts, "If you buy a Hebrew servant, six years shall he serve." This means that the soul may come back to this world six times to correct its deficiencies. There is another opinion that says the soul may come back three or four times. This number is derived from another Bible verse (Exod. 20:5). "The sins of the fathers are revisited to the third and fourth generations."

People often question if this is fair. Kabbalah says that the sin is not passed on to innocent children, but it is the same soul who comes back in the third and fourth generations of the family to correct its deficiencies. If the soul fails to complete its mission within four to six reincarnations, it is possible that it may have to reincarnate as an animal, vegetable or stone. This is a punishment, for it is the hardest reincarnation.

A part of the soul of every person has been here before. When we die and the soul separates from the body, it enters into a plane of existence for review and purification that generally lasts eleven months, according to Jewish belief. At this time, the family members say a prayer that is known as *Kaddish*. This prayer offers protection and healing for the departed soul. We are told that the soul greatly appreciates these prayers for it is not capable of performing any good deeds that would protect and uplift it. Therefore, whatever good deeds people do in the memory of the departed soul help it greatly. It is customary for people to learn Torah and make charitable contributions in the memory of the departed.

If a soul leaves this world pure and unsullied, it does not have to reincarnate. The *Zohar* says that the soul is kept for the body it has left until the time of resurrection. Until then, the soul enters what is known as the "Palace of Love," which the *Zohar* describes as the place where "all the treasures of the King are stored and all his love kisses are." This is a time of ecstasy. Unfortunately, many souls remain there a very short time. Often reincarnation is against the will and desire of the soul.

Reincarnation is a gift, but in my estimation it seems like a booby prize. It would be better for the soul to stay in the spiritual world. My feelings reflect the views of some sages in the Talmud who state, "It would be better not to be born." Nevertheless, being here in the physical world offers a great opportunity for the soul to correct its deficiencies, to do *mitzvot,* so that when it returns to the spiritual world it will enjoy a higher goodness. It can also be a beautiful experience, as well as fun, to inhabit a physical body. In some cases, the soul volunteers to return to this world because it wants to be of service to others, particularly to the people with whom it has past-life connections, such as a spouse.

Reincarnation enters into selection of a marriage partner. We do not marry anyone we did not know before, yet it sometimes happens that the people we marry may not be our true soul mates. It takes great merit to marry our true soul mate. According to the Talmud, a person's first marriage is predestined. The *Zohar* says that if a man did not marry or have children in his lifetime because he purposely avoided performing the *mitzvah* to be fruitful and multiply, he will have to be punished and will reincarnate. A woman is under no obligation, however, to bear children and will not suffer in the next lifetime if she does not do so. If a man was married to a woman who was his true soul mate and they could not have children, they will reincarnate together again and have children. They will never marry anyone else and will easily recognize each other in the next lifetime.

The *Zohar* describes in detail the dangers of marrying a widow because of reincarnation. If the man dies first and the woman remarries, the *Zohar* says that there will be a struggle between the soul of the first husband and that of the second. The soul of the first husband will come to the woman in dreams and will try to make her stay bonded to him. If she continues to miss her first husband, she will not be able to bond deeply with the second. If the second husband prevails and the woman is happy with him and does bond with him, the soul of the first husband will retreat from her and return to the Palace of Love. If, however, the soul of the first husband was her true soul mate, he will not depart from her, and the second husband might die if he stays married to her. The *Zohar* cautions people to be wary when marrying a widow or widower because they cannot know for sure whether the first spouse was the true soul mate.

According to the *Zohar,* it may even be dangerous to be married to a person who is not your soul mate, even though it happens all the time. If the true soul mate of the spouse prays hard to be united with his or her mate, the person who is not the true soul mate may become ill and die. It is best to be divorced from a person who is not your soul mate than to die. These teachings have been a comfort for me personally. Shortly after getting married, just a few years ago, I became deathly ill. It was very frightening and a very painful experience for me. As I was recuperating from the illness and regaining my health, my husband divorced me. He did not want to work on the marriage. I was devastated. It did not seem fair. It seemed so cruel. I had married late in life, and I thought that my first husband was my true soul mate, the one I had waited so long for in this lifetime— and perhaps countless lifetimes before. I gave my whole heart and soul to the marriage. Now, as I continue to learn these teachings of kabbalah, I accept that everything happened as it did because my first husband was not my soul mate. God spared me. I am so glad that I lived and now pray to be reunited soon with my true soul mate.

The *Zohar* comments that male and female souls are two parts of the same soul. They search for each other, and when they have sufficient merit they marry. Hopefully, one of them will not already be married to another person when the other becomes ready or worthy to marry. This can be a delicate problem. Many people do not merit marrying their true soul mate, and they can be happily married to another person who is not their soul mate. One of the partners does not necessarily have to die. The *Zohar* says that marriage is permitted between people who are not soul mates because children will emerge from this union and the couple were not yet worthy to marry their true soul mates.

In some cases it is better for a couple that are not soul mates to divorce. Still, divorce may not free a person to marry his or her true soul mate if the person failed to learn from the previous marriage to heal or fix what was intended with the spouse. However, if a couple completed what they were supposed to do or could do with each other, divorce might allow them to be available to marry their true soul mates. If a person is in doubt about whether they should marry or stay married, they should consult a kabbalist or a *tzaddik* for guidance. There are people in the community of Israel who can answer these soul questions.

If a couple stay together for their lifetime and do not divorce, they will reincarnate and marry their true soul mates in the next lifetime. For some people there is only one soul mate. They often find each other early in life. For most people there are many soul mates. There are many people we may love, many people with whom we are soul mates of some sort, but we will not marry them all. Yet they are soul mates because our soul is made more whole by the connection with them. The purposes and intensities of soul connections vary.

Kabbalah says that the female soul often completes her karma more quickly than a male soul. Often, the female soul reincarnates in the physical world not because she needs to rectify something but solely to be with her beloved, to help him and others. Rabbi Yitzchok Luria said that sometimes a woman reincarnates just for the opportunity to marry the soul mate because he may not have been worthy enough to marry her in previous lifetimes. I imagine that some women will be happy to hear this mystical statement about a female soul being so elevated and pure. As a channel of giving in the world, her primary purpose is to lift up her beloved. Those of a more feminist orientation may find this objectionable, for it implies that a woman's main and primary purpose is to be married.

As I learn more about reincarnation, I can see how the knowledge of it can be problematic and why its exploration was discouraged. Reincarnation can offer a perspective that may be comforting, but it may also be used in negative ways. For example, knowing that our suffering is an atonement for past sins may be a source of comfort. With this knowledge, we may more easily accept our situation with a sense of equanimity. We accept the destiny of our lives if we believe that it is our fate and there is a purpose to it. However, believing in reincarnation might also foster passivity in our life, allowing us to remain in a negative situation when we need not do so. It is hard to have the spiritual clarity to know whether suffering comes from past-life circumstances or from this lifetime.

Belief in reincarnation could also be used as an excuse to withhold help from others. We could easily say that other people's suffering is their karma, the result of their actions, from another lifetime. I actually heard people say this when I was visiting India. Past-life karma was used as a rationale for allowing people to live in squalor and poverty. I cannot believe this is what God truly wants. It may be other people's karma that they are suffering, but it is our privilege and responsibility to help them if we can. And we are judged by what we do and do not do. If we are idle in the presence of the suffering of others, we may find ourselves abandoned by others when we suffer. Generally speaking, we must do whatever we can to lift ourselves and others up and accept with equanimity the things that we cannot change. We all have the mission to rectify ourselves, others and the world.

There is a tendency to use the ideas about reincarnation inappropriately in regard to marriage. A person may justify running away from a challenging marriage by claiming that the spouse is not the true soul mate. This may not be true at all. Marriage to our soul mate is not always sweet. Such a marriage may be more challenging. It is hard to know for sure that the person you marry is your true soul mate. As stated, many people do not actually marry their soul mates, but that does not mean that they do not have karma with the person they are married to or that they should have waited for their true soul mates. As a general rule, you have past-life karma with whomever you marry.

Kabbalah discusses two other variations of reincarnation, *ibur* and *dybbuk*. The phenomenon of *ibur,* "pregnancy," refers to the partial incarnation, a spark of the soul of a *tzaddik* entering a living person. Usually a person is rewarded with an *ibur* after much spiritual striving. An *ibur* becomes part of the person. It does not feel like an alien being. An *ibur* happens suddenly, without preparation. Suddenly, a person sees and knows things he did not know before. It may be a transient experience or a more lasting one. The transformation in the person may or may not be obvious to others. If a person commits sins, the *ibur* will leave. Having an *ibur* is a precious gift.

The other, less pleasant variation is that of *dybbuk*. A *dybbuk* is the soul of another that invades a person as an alien force intermittently or continually. There are movies and tales about this phenomenon, as well as many stories of the exorcism of a *dybbuk,* and they are not just folklore. Some of these stories border on the bizarre. I read that Rav Kook of Israel expelled a *dybbuk* on several occasions. It is possible that a person may seem to be mentally ill, and even be diagnosed as such, but in truth he may have a *dybbuk* bothering him. Some violent crimes may be committed by people who have a *dybbuk*. The *dybbuk* is a damaged soul, full of negative energy. This soul seeks to belong and tries to attach itself to whatever it can. It feels homeless and is in a terrible state of limbo. The host of the *dybbuk* is generally a person who does not connect with God, being weak or negative. Having a *dybbuk* is painful. The soul needs to be exorcised for the sake of both people. Some *tzaddikim* specialize in this kind of exorcism for they know the secret of spiritual unification: how to unite the letters of God's name with the person's name so that the *dybbuk* departs.

14

HOLIJTIC HEALING

Holistic healing is emerging as a viable and popular way of treating physical and emotional illnesses. Associated with New Age thinking, holistic healing recognizes the interplay of body, mind and spirit. With the traditional medical model, people who are ill are directed to numerous specialists who have expertise about a particular part of the body or a particular disease. The medical orientation that has prevailed in Western culture is to eradicate the disease or the symptoms as they are manifested. Medical doctors who follow this model prescribe drugs to mask or control symptoms, an approach that sometimes creates other symptoms as side effects. Such doctors are not trained to address the role that nutrition, emotional stress, environmental pollution and electromagnetic fields play in the formation of disease.

The holistic approach is quite different. True holistic doctors or health practitioners do not treat the isolated symptoms that a person presents but rather the whole person. They account for the role that nutrition and personal and environmental stress play in the formation of disease. There are many different kinds of holistic health practitioners. Using a variety of natural modalities, such as homeopathy, acupuncture, vitamins, herbs, diet, meditation, prayer and counseling, holistic health practitioners work to restore and strengthen the body's immune system and life force. A good practitioner recognizes the roles of both spirituality and psychology in the healing of a person. The body is not considered to be a separate entity with its own pathology. Rather, what happens in the body is a manifestation of what is happening in the nonphysical parts of a person. Regardless of the specialty of the holistic practitioner or healer, all seek to restore harmony to the body and soul. To experience greater levels of health, a person must make a variety of lifestyle, emotional and spiritual changes to support the natural healing processes of the body. It is not enough to take a pill, even if it is a vitamin or an herb. It requires commitment and dedication and intention.

Dr. Donald Epstein, the founder of Network Chiropractic treatment, sums it up this way: "Practitioners who focus on the symptoms miss the whole point. Diseases don't make people sick. They are the result of being sick, therefore focusing on the disease will not make people well. You have to take a look at what fundamentally went wrong in that body to allow that condition to exist. Wellness cannot be added to the body in the form of an injection or pill. It comes from within. You have to remove the obstructions to the body's own inherent wisdom, the only power that makes you well."

Holistic healing is not a new approach. It is strikingly similar to the Jewish understanding of disease and health. Judaism teaches that the essence of a person is the soul, which for a brief period of time, in the context of eternity, is connected to a physical body. Health is the perfect harmony of the body and the soul. According to kabbalah, there are five levels of the soul (see chapter 4). On the lowest level, _nefesh,_ the soul animates the body. On the next level, _ruach,_ the soul arouses the heart, giving us the capacity to feel. On the next level, _neshama,_ the soul gives us the capacity to think and to perceive holiness. The other two levels, _chaya_ and _yehida,_ are outside the body and connect directly to God. The soul of a person is within and surrounding the body. When we do good deeds, when we are loving and compassionate, when we learn Torah, when we meditate, we infuse soul energy into the various levels of the soul within our bodies and connect the surrounding soul to the soul that is within the body. As we learned, *mitzvah,* a good deed, means "to connect."

The body receives its spiritual nourishment from the soul through its good thoughts, feelings and acts. The body cannot function if not for the life-force energy of the soul. According to kabbalah, it is the soul that gives the eyes the ability to see, the ears the ability to hear, etc. If the soul were to fully enter into and be tied to the body, we would live forever. When the soul separates from the body, we die. When the body and soul enjoy the proper partnership, a person is healthy. Most of the practices of Judaism are directed to making this unification between the body and the soul. For example, we make blessings before and after eating. In this way, eating becomes an elevated spiritual experience that brings unification between the soul and the body rather than becoming a physical, animalistic act. Blessing food also helps us to be conscious about the selection of the foods that we eat, reminding us to eat the most natural, life-sustaining foods.

According to Rabbi Hayim Vital, God made the body to clothe the soul according to the anatomy of the soul. Corresponding to the pre-scribed 613 commandments, the body has 248 spiritual limbs and 365 spiritual sinews that are clothed inside the physical limbs and function like pipes to bring blood and life-force energy to the body. Vital wrote in book three of *Shaane Kedusha, Gates of Holiness,* "Every limb from the 248 limbs is given substance by a *mitzvah* which corresponds to that limb." Vital commented that what is even more nourishing and important are the *middot* (the qualities) of a person: "Through our emotional qualities we connect our souls and Godliness to our physical bodies. Or we disconnect. If we are over-come with anger and jealousy, the soul begins to depart. By our negative thoughts, speech, and actions, we set up blocks, barriers between the flow of soul energy into the body." When we become more proficient in meditative kabbalah, we are able to detect exactly the location of the blockages in the flow and provide spiritual medi-tative remedies to strengthen the flow of the soul energy into the body.

Disease begins in the spiritual dimension. If the disease is not attended to there, it will manifest on the physical level, forcing us to take note of the disharmony between the body and the soul. According to Judaism and kabbalah, illness is caused by a weakening of the soul's power to animate the body. The *Tanya* says that we get sick when something goes wrong in the circulation of life-force energy within us. The Tzemach Tzedek, the successor of the Alter Rebbe in the Lubavitch lineage, said that sickness comes from stagnation. The animal soul, which desires pure physicality, stops the godly soul from cleaving to God, the source of all energy and healing. Rabbi Nachman said that when the soul sees that the person is not carrying out God's Will, it begins to leave the body. As the power of the soul is weakened, the person becomes sick. The Talmud states that anger is considered a sin worse than worshipping idols. When people become angry, according to Hayim Vital, it causes a separation between the lower and higher levels of soul. People then become confused about who they are or depressed about who they think they might be.

The rabbis of the Talmud taught that illness comes from sin. What is sin? Sin does not mean that a person is inherently bad or evil but rather that he made a mistake that resulted in a blockage that prohibited the flow of goodness from the divine connection. Separation from God may occur on the physical level by doing acts that are against Divine Will. Sin may occur on the emotional level by dwelling on such negative feelings as jealousy or anger, or it may occur on the mental level by believing in forces other than God.

Interestingly, the Bible stipulates that a person fast as penance for committing various sins. Because people today are physically weaker than people of the past, we do not fast as penance for our sins. Yet a friend of mine went to a special medical facility recently to undergo a supervised water-only fast of forty days. She reported that people came from all over the country to heal themselves of a variety of illnesses through fasting. And she saw many amazing happenings in the short time she was there. Fasting is being rediscovered as a cure for many diseases and illnesses, including cancer and heart disease. Not only does the body have the time to release toxins and heal through fasting, but without the distraction of food the individual also has a greater opportunity to do *teshuvah* through introspection. I caution people considering fasting for healing that they do so under the supervision of experienced medical or naturo-pathic doctors.

Judaism teaches that the purpose of all suffering is either to make people turn to God or to cleanse them of former sins so they will be able to absorb more goodness into their lives. It is best not to dwell on reasons for becoming ill for that may lead to despair and self-pity. Rather, we should focus on how to heal and become better than we were before. When we are fully recovered from an illness and no longer in pain, we may better understand the role that illness played in our becoming a better person.

If the soul is fulfilling the purpose for which it came into this world, it is happy and the person is healthy. The lack of knowing and/or fulfilling our life purpose may bring on feelings of anxiety, despair, depression and/or many psychosomatic conditions. In her book *Why People Don't Heal and How They Can,* Carolyn Myss gives numerous examples of people becoming ill when they were not ful-filling their life purpose. For example, a person may be doing work that he hates, be married to a person he doesn't love and who doesn't love him, and not even be aware of how he is hurting him-self. Getting sick is a message from his body that he needs to look at his life. Don't blame yourself for becoming ill. Rather, learn from the experience. In the process of healing, you may make important life changes that align you more closely with your divine purpose. Illness may be a blessing in disguise when it becomes a vehicle for transformation. People often make wonderful changes in their lives because of illness and are happier and more fulfilled than before.

All healing is considered a form of *teshuvah,* which is the return to the essential natural self that is healthy and vital (see chapter 9). The Tzemach Tzedek said that in turning to God, we go beyond the world of cause and effect and are thus able to draw down the high-est healing energy. The soul has the ability to channel this healing energy to the body through prayer and meditation. It is vital that a sick person turn to God for all healing comes from Him. Healing is a matter of getting plugged into the flow of divine blessing.

There is a story told about King Hezekiah, a ruler of ancient Israel. He was a righteous man and was told by the prophet Isaiah that he would die soon. King Hezekiah then examined himself deeply and pleaded with God to let him live. God listened to him, and the king lived and corrected the deficiencies that had led to his illness. The *midrash* says that an ancient *Book of Remedies* contained information about how to heal all illnesses. King Hezekiah who had healed himself through *teshuvah,* by turning to God and changing himself, thought the remedies were too effective. He was concerned that people would rely on the remedies and not on God, so he buried this wisdom. He wanted people to have the opportunity to use illness to become better people and not to settle for an alleviation of their symptoms. Unfortunately, this information is now lost to us.

Judaism has always emphasized faith in God, and faith in God is the best medicine. God is the true healer, and all healing comes from God. If we are sick, we should do *teshuvah* and examine the ways in which we have blocked the divine flow of goodness in our lives. Oftentimes, that is hard to do. Sick people need to look at the anger they feel in their lives and release and transform it. They should make an effort to correct what is in their power to do and work to increase their trust and faith in God. People, however, must be honest with themselves about where they stand regarding trust in God.

There are levels of trust in God. Totally righteous people can rely on God alone for everything. They have no doubt that God will answer their prayers in the best possible way. It is enough for them to pray for healing. People with less faith may pray to and place their faith in *tzaddikim. Tzaddikim* can help provide the blessings that people would be incapable of receiving on their own. In former days, people would turn to the prophets, not to doctors, if they were ill. Throughout Jewish history, there have been many great miraculous healers. Most of the Chassidic rebbes were herbalists and spiritual healers. When I was very sick several years ago, I was most helped by a spiritual healer from Israel.

There are many stories about the healing powers of rebbes. Here is one of my favorites: A man collapses. His wife runs to a great rebbe and the rebbe tells her, "Give your husband coffee." She gives her husband coffee, and he becomes well. Months go by and her husband becomes ill once again and the wife runs to the rebbe. The rebbe tells her to give him coffee. She gives him coffee, and again he becomes well. Time passes and the husband becomes sick again. The wife thinks she will save a trip to the rebbe, so she gives her husband coffee as the rebbe always recommends. The man's health continues to deteriorate. The wife runs to the rebbe and tells him that she has given him coffee.

The rebbe exclaims in utter disbelief and astonishment, "You gave him coffee!"

"What shall I do?" she cries.

The rebbe replies, "Give him coffee."

She goes home, gives her husband coffee, and he regains his health. They realize the coffee was only a container for the blessing of the rebbe. Without the blessing, the man could not be healed.

In recent times, the Lubavitcher Rebbe healed many, many people miraculously. I have heard numerous personal accounts of people who followed the rebbe's instructions to trust in God and not have an operation mandated by medical doctors. A man I met at a personal growth workshop I attended years ago told me that the Lubavitcher Rebbe had told his mother not to have the hysterectomy her doctors ordered to save her life. At the time, I was surprised that the Lubavitcher Rebbe told her not to listen to her doctors. Not listening to one's doctor takes great faith. The woman followed the rebbe's advice and went on to have five sons. Though the Lubavitcher Rebbe is no longer in the physical body, going to his grave is very healing and powerful.

If we do not have perfect faith ourselves or in a *tzaddik,* we should be honest with ourselves and seek the best medical doctors we can find and pray that God will work through them. It is always a good idea to ask people to pray for you as well. According to kabbalah, healing is actually ministered through angels. Angels are God's messengers of healing. Even if we go to doctors, we should always be mindful that our healing comes from God. The Gemara says that all doctors have angels with them who inspire healing. A doctor reputed to have healing powers has a greater angel working in tandem. I personally recommend that people turn to alternative healers such as acupuncturists, chiropractors, naturopaths, spiritual energy healers, herbalists and others, along with medical doctors. They are often more attuned to angelic healing energies.

A great deal of current research validates the role that faith and
prayer play in healing. Several studies funded by the John
Templeton Foundation have shown that patients who had religious
faith were three times more likely to survive heart operations. Heart
patients who are religious have postoperative hospital stays that are
20 percent shorter than those of nonreligious patients. A study that
followed over two thousand people for six years found that people
over sixty-five years of age who regularly participated in religious
activities were 40 percent less likely to have high blood pressure.
According to the Templeton report, family physicians are increasingly cognizant of the power of faith and spirituality to affect the
healing process. For over twenty-five years, pioneering studies by
Dr. Herbert Benson have shown the power of meditation for healing.
Thanks to Benson's efforts, meditation is now offered to heart, cancer and AIDS patients at the Mind/Body Medical Institute of Harvard
University.

Prayer has traditionally and universally been recognized as a powerful instrument for healing. In his wonderful book _Healing Words,_
Dr. Larry Dossey presented scientific documentation of the power of
prayer. He cited one study where heart patients were divided into
two groups. One group was prayed for; the other was not. Neither
group was aware of the study. The group that was prayed for recu-
perated significantly quicker.

It is a very rewarding practice to pray for the healing of others.
Traditional Jewish prayer services contains certain times when
prayers for healing are offered. It is customary during these prayers
to say the person's name, the name of the person's parents ("daughter of" or "son of") and the person's mother's Hebrew name. I say the
people's names and visualize them with my eyes closed. I reflect on
the pain they are facing, how they really need this blessing. I then
ask God to shine His Light and love on them. God is always radiating light and love, but sometimes we are not open to receiving it.

When I pray for others, I imagine that I bring these people to God
and that they are open to receive God's Light and love. I see them
happy and healthy and surrounded by God's Light. I thank God for
healing them. I then say the final blessing: "Blessed are You, _Adonoy,_
who heals the sick." Have faith in the blessing you have made. It is

important that you believe the healing has occurred.

I know people who have been concerned that if they prayed for others, they would use up their "account" with God. The opposite is true. The more you pray for others, the more God listens to your prayers for yourself.

A little known and powerful kabbalistic practice for healing that is from the Arizel, Rabbi Yitzchok Luria, is to interlace the letters of the Divine Name with the *holom* (oh) vowel—the *yud,* the *hay,* the *vav,* and the *hay,* so the letters become *yoh, hoh, voh* and *hoh*—with the letters of the sick person's name. For example, if you are praying for a person with the name Sarah, you would write *Yoh, Soh, Hoh, Roh, Voh, Hoh, Hoh.* If the name contains more letters than the Divine Name does, start again with another round of the Divine Name letters. When you pray for this person, look at what you have written. You may even say this permutation of the Divine Name silently to yourself as you pray for healing for this person.

In Judaism, charity is considered to be a powerful vehicle for healing. In his book of teachings, *Likutey Moharan,* Rabbi Nachman said, "It is through charity that all blessing flows into the world. . . . Charity is the remedy for all wounds." By giving charity we become a greater vessel, more worthy of receiving blessings. It is said that by giving charity we sweeten the judgments against us. If we give money to a *tzaddik* who will pray for us, this is the best because this obligates the *tzaddik.*

There is yet another ancient Jewish healing practice of changing the name of a person who is suffering from a life-threatening illness. According to kabbalah, a name is not just something that a person is called; rather, it is a reflection of inner essence. A person's name has a certain destiny attached to it. When we change the name, we change the destiny. Often we add a name that then gives additional life force to the person. When my grandmother was three years old, she was very ill. She was taken to the Vishnitzer Rebbe for a blessing. Her name was changed, and she lived to see me until I was three years old. I wonder if the Vishnitzer Rebbe blessed her by saying that she would see a grandchild who reached the age of three.

In addition to being a great elucidator of Jewish law and philosophy, the Rambam (Maimonides) was a physician and forerunner of the holistic health movement. He stated very definitively that if people would follow his recommendations for diet and exercise, they would not become ill. Because the Rambam was emphatic about this, I thought it important to include in this chapter some of his recommendations:

1. You should not eat to the point of satiation, but only until the stomach is three-quarters full.
2. You should not drink water while eating, except for a little mixed with wine. When the food begins to be digested, you may drink, but not to excess.
3. You should not eat until you have relieved yourself and should never delay in doing so. You should have loose bowel movements and do what is necessary to have loose bowels. Constipation is a sign of illness.
4. You should not eat until you have walked or engaged in some form of physical exertion to the point that the body has become warm. As a general rule, you should subdue the body and exert yourself every morning. You should rest a bit until composure has been regained and then eat.
5. When you eat, you should sit or recline on your left side in one place. You should not walk or ride or exert yourself, nor should you move about or take a stroll until your food has been digested. Those who are accustomed to walking about or exerting themselves immediately after eating will bring severe illnesses upon themselves.
6. You should not sleep on the front or the back but on the side. At the beginning of the night, you should sleep on the left side and at the end of the night on the right. You should not sleep directly after eating, but should wait three or four hours. You should avoid sleeping during the day.
7. Foods that enhance the process of digestion, such as grapes, figs, berries, pears, melons, squash and cucumbers, should be consumed at the beginning of a meal. They should not be combined with substantial foods. Rather, you should wait after eating them until they have passed through the stomach and then proceed to the meal itself.
8. A person who wishes to eat poultry and meat in the same meal

should eat the poultry first and then the meat. You should always eat the lighter food first.

The Rambam made many other recommendations regarding foods we should or should not eat. Examples include the following: We should eat grapes, figs and almonds. We should avoid or limit the intake of carob, dried fruits, lentils, salted fish or cheeses, and mushrooms.

The Rambam particularly emphasized the importance of exercise. He said that if we exercise a lot, do not overeat, and have frequent and loose bowel movements, we will not become sick, even if our diet is bad. Similarly, those who eat good food but do not exercise will be sickly and weak. This is also true for children.

The Rambam also said that every plant has healing properties. Some plants have healing properties we do not yet know, but we will find a use for every plant in time. In the Bible, God says, "Before they call, I will answer." God created the disease but He also gave the cure. The Rambam said that the cures for all our illnesses will come from ordinary places. I recommend that people learn about the wonderful properties of herbs and foods. They can be very effective in healing and not have the side effects associated with prescription medicines.

In my private practice, I work as a holistic and spiritual healer. People come to me privately for meditation therapy because they are experiencing physical symptoms, such as high blood pressure, fatigue, colitis, cancer and migraines, or emotional problems, such as anxiety, depression and bipolar disorders. They have heard that meditation strengthens the immune system, reduces stress and promotes a greater sense of well-being, and they want to learn how to meditate within a Jewish framework.

I would like to share with you how I work with people privately because it may provide some guidance to anyone who is ill or who wishes to better understand a more holistic way of healing. When I first see someone, I assess where the person is physically, emotionally and spiritually. I identify the strengths and the weaknesses on all levels. We have to know where we are if we want to grow. From my holistic perspective, I suggest that disease manifests on all levels of being. People who are physically ill are often closed spiritually, think negative thoughts, have lots of unresolved feelings, and may be engaged in destructive or unhealthy behaviors. I work on all three levels—mind, body, emotions—with the awareness that whatever is done on one level impacts the other levels as well.

It is easiest to intervene on the physical level. The first thing I do with all my clients is examine their breathing patterns and teach them how to breathe fully and deeply. People who are not well or who are stressed do not breathe correctly. Deep breathing promotes healing. The human body discharges toxins through breathing. Deep breathing allows for the maximum intake of oxygen and release of carbon dioxide. The blood is reoxygenated. Digestion is aided. Blood pressure is lowered. Deep breathing also reduces stress and enhances mental concentration and physical performance. Deep breathing has many benefits. I do not think people will feel better until they learn how to take slow, deep and full breaths. As a healer, I then look at diet, exercise patterns and body posture. Most people suffering from physical or emotional illnesses are not eating as well as they could. I recommend that people augment their diets to increase the intake of organic vegetables, whole grains and fresh juices, and eliminate sugar, caffeine, chocolate, wheat and processed foods.

All too often I have had clients who have been given medication without a review of their diet. I recently saw a woman who was given medication for high blood pressure. The doctor failed to note that her diet consisted of a great deal of cheese, soy sauce—which contains salt—and processed foods, all of which contribute to high blood pressure. She was willing to make dietary changes, but her doctor preferred to give her medication. Earlier in this book, I mentioned the woman suffering for years with migraines who was addicted to chocolate, which is known to trigger migraines. If people would change their diets, relax and learn how to feel better about themselves, in most cases they would be healthier and happier. They most likely would not need medications, which often have toxic side effects. It behooves everyone who is experiencing a physical or emotional problem to help themselves holistically.

In addition to changing diet, people need to exercise if they want to feel well. Building up a sweat is the best thing to do because perspiration releases toxins. In *Likutey Moharan II*, Reb Nachman said, "The remedy is to sweat, because the illness-generating toxins in the blood are exuded in the sweat, and the blood is left pure. One can then come to joy. The reason is because depression is caused by the build-up of impurities in the blood and the spleen." We also gain vitality by moving our bodies. Be sure that you begin exercising gradually and under the guidance of a doctor, especially if you have pre-existing medical conditions. We also need to drink lots of pure water, and do at least ten minutes of deep breathing outside each day. These simple recommendations will make a difference in your life. Our bodies have tremendous healing capabilities if we do these simple things to support ourselves.

Our relationships play a significant role in our health and illness. Just as a person may act out the pain in the family or derive secondary gains from other people by being sick, good loving relationships can actually heal people. In his book *Reversing Heart Disease,* Dr. Dean Ornish identified many studies documenting that physical healing was expedited by the disclosure of feelings to other people. Individuals in group therapy live longer than people who remain isolated. Ornish concluded that isolation leads to illness and intimacy to health. Judaism has always emphasized the *mitzvah* of visiting the sick, known in Hebrew as *bikur cholim.* The Talmud says that a person who visits the sick takes away a sixtieth of the ill person's pain. The rabbis then ask if sixty people visit a sick person, would this person be healed? In the *midrash,* Rabbi Huna said that total healing happens only if the sixty visitors love the patient as their own souls. But even without this, the pain of a sick person will be relieved.

I conclude this chapter with a testimony to the healing power of love. Like most Chassidic tales, this story is itself a spiritual transmission of healing.

A person destined to become a rebbe would travel among the people disguised as a poor person so he could learn about their lives. One such future rebbe, Mendel Rizhiner, left home at the age of fourteen. On his travels he met a young girl of six named Sarah. Outside her home, on the road, she had a little table with a few surrounding chairs where she greeted passersby. She invited Mendel to join her and happily fed him some food and drink. After feeding him, she danced around him.

"What is your name?" she asked him.

"My name is Mendel," he replied.

Whenever he was in her town, he would visit her. She would offer him a snack and drink and then she would sing and dance around him with great joy. After two years of traveling, Mendel returned to his father's home and five or six years later he became a rebbe to thousands of people. His fame as a rebbe and as a healer spread throughout the country. Many people claimed to be healed by his blessings.

Around the same time, Sarah was stricken with a mysterious illness that left her paralyzed. Though her parents took her to various doctors, she could not be helped. Like everyone in the town, she had heard about the famous miracle worker, Rebbe Mendel Rizhiner. She asked her parents to take her to see the rebbe. "Maybe he will be able to heal me." She sensed in her heart that the famous rebbe was really her old friend Mendel. She knew it, but her parents laughed when she told them. Though she begged them to take her to see him, they refused.

They told her, "It is a long, hard journey there, and if we went most likely we would not be given the chance to see the rebbe. And if we are given the chance to see the rebbe, most likely the rebbe will not be able to heal you. And most likely the rebbe is not your friend Mendel. And if he is, most likely he will not remember you. The whole journey will accomplish nothing, and it will be very hard on everyone."

They said everything they could to discourage her, yet she continued to beg them. When it appeared that they would not listen to her cries, she told them with a conviction well beyond her years, "I will go to see the rebbe, even if I have to crawl there myself."

Sensing her strong determination, and perhaps fearing the embarrassment she would cause them by crawling through the town, her parents consented to take her to see the rebbe. Throughout the journey, they told her that the rebbe would not see her, that he would not be able to heal her and that he would not remember her. "Don't expect too much. We do not want you to be disappointed," they continually told her.

Just as they arrived in the town, the rebbe told some of his followers that they would have a special guest and should prepare a table and chairs and some food and drink. In no time at all, the Chassidim saw the young girl being wheeled in a cart to the rebbe's house. "This must be the special guest the rebbe was talking about." They ran to greet her, telling her and her parents that the rebbe was expecting her. She was quickly ushered into the room where the table and chairs had been prepared for her.

The rebbe soon entered and greeted her warmly. "Oh, Sarah, I am so happy to see you, but I am so sorry to see that you are suffering." He started crying to God, "I can't bear to see Sarah suffering like this. I can't bear it. I can't bear it." He said this several times, sobbing with each word. "Please heal her now." He begged of God from the deepest place in his heart and soul. Finally, he composed himself and said to Sarah, "Remember how you used to feed me when you were young? I want you to bring me some food now." With not too much struggle, Sarah got up and fed the rebbe. She was healed.

Though we may not be on the level of this rebbe or have access to such rebbes, in our own way we can be rebbes to our friends by providing a truly compassionate listening presence in their times of distress. We can help to heal other people through our love. If we can cry for people and, better yet, cry with them, we can heal them, even if they never recover from the illness. Our tears open the gates of heaven. Healing may not be the same as curing. Healing is about becoming whole, regaining a sense of well-being.

In working with a lot of people with physical illness or emotional disorders, I have come to feel that many illnesses begin simply because there was no one in their lives to truly love them and really be there with them with all the feelings they carry inside. Having our feelings acknowledged and validated is healing and empowering. Sometimes clients will tell me about the most horrific things they endured without shedding a tear. When I listen to their stories, I sense how they have been hurt very deeply, and I tell them so. Sometimes I will shed tears as I talk to them. By doing so, I hope I can communicate to them that it is safe and healing to feel their pain.

There are many meditations that promote physical and emotional healing. People who are troubled cannot heal themselves by living, feeling and thinking in their usual or habitual manner. They have to go beyond the ego mind for healing. Talking about their problems and their pain is not enough. They need to feel their feelings, whatever they may be, and quiet the mind so they can hear their own soul, the transcendent and deepest part of themselves. They have to make a commitment to their own healing and learn to love themselves. They must make a God-connection. If they cannot make this connection themselves, they need to find people who can help them to do so. The speed of healing intensifies when we truly see and acknowledge that our pain is a wake-up call from God.

I view illness as a spiritual initiation, a call for greater service and God-consciousness. Through the process of being ill, we have an opportunity to become better than before. In my work with people, I basically help them make the direct connection to God so they can receive the healing they need. God is a master healer.

15

JEWISH VEGETARIANISM

Vegetarianism, long associated with the New Age, has a strong basis in Judaism and kabbalah. Vegetarianism is becoming more popular and mainstream largely because it has tremendous health benefits. Meat consumption has been associated with heart disease, cancer, kidney disease, hypertension and much more. In his book *Reversing Heart Disease*, Dr. Dean Ornish cited a position paper from the American Dietetic Association that reported, "A considerable body of scientific data suggest positive relationships between vegetarian lifestyles and risk reduction for several chronic degenerative diseases and conditions such as obesity, coronary artery disease, hypertension, diabetes mellitus, colon cancer, and others. Vegetarians also have lower rates of osteoporosis, lung cancer, breast cancer, kidney stones, and diverticular disease."

Dr. Ornish documented the effectiveness of a vegetarian diet, coupled with meditation and group support, in actually reversing heart disease. Not only can heart disease be reversed in this way, but optimal health can be maintained, in contrast to the more expensive bypass surgery or balloon angioplasty, which alleviate symptoms for only a brief time.

To make matters worse, nowadays cows, steers and lambs are fed

hormones and antibiotics and drink water contaminated with pesti-
cide residues that remain active in the meat we consume. The general practice of using antibiotics indiscriminately to boost animals'
growth and keep them alive in today's slaughterhouses has led to the
rise of resistant bacteria. The increase in consumption of antibiotics
by animals and humans contributes to the need for more powerful
and newer antibiotics as we increase our tolerance to current antibiotics. A report issued in July 1997 by the National Research Council,
a government advisory body, stated that cases of antibiotic-resistant
human disease caused from livestock have "clearly occurred." A
study published in the *New England Journal of Medicine* in May
1998 estimated that between 68,000 and 340,000 Americans are
infected each year with DT104, a strain of salmonella that is already
resistant to five antibiotics. Many more food-poisoning incidents,
such as those caused by *E. coli,* are attributed directly to meat consumption. Meat also contains pesticides. According to a report from
the Viva Vegie Society, an advocacy group for vegetarianism, animals contain fourteen times more pesticides than plant foods.
Pesticides have been implicated in cancer and other immune-
disorder diseases.

Today, most animals are raised for slaughter in small, crowded
cages and eat food laced with antibiotics and hormones. They cannot walk around, enjoy the outdoors, be petted or loved. They are
raised specifically for food. This factory mentality has negative consequences for us as well as for the animals. Exercise is very important
for animals. In his wonderful book, *Judaism and Vegetarianism,*
Richard Schwartz reported that when animals are denied exercise,
as generally occurs with today's factory methods, their metabolism
is altered and their meat becomes infested with waste, which would
have disappeared had the animals been allowed to exercise. Judaism
asks us to safeguard our health. Without our health, we cannot serve
God. In light of the above, it behooves people to limit their consumption of meat.

Even though many people are attracted to vegetarianism to refrain
from and counteract the cruelty associated with animal slaughter,
many others are unaware of the current practices by which animals
are raised and killed for consumption. Jews like to think that if the

animal has been slaughtered according to Jewish law and is deemed
kosher that the animal has not suffered, but this is not true.
Nowadays, the kosher animal you eat has suffered tremendously.
The Torah has always emphasized compassion to animals, yet compassion is not practiced in Jewish slaughterhouses. The animals are
not treated differently from how they are treated in any slaughter-
house. The Torah states that animals should be free to graze in the
fields ("And I will give grass in thy fields for the cattle."—Deut.
11:15) and to rest on the Sabbath ("Remember the Sabbath day to
keep it holy. Six days shall thou work, but the seventh day is a
Sabbath unto the Lord thy God. In it thou should not do any manner of work, thou, nor thy son, nor thy daughter, nor thy man servant nor thy maid servant nor thy cattle, nor thy stranger that is
within thy gates."—Exod. 20:8–10). But today animals remain confined to cages, eating waste products, chemicals and hormones.
They do not graze in the pastures. This is not how the Torah mandates the treatment of animals.

Many other Torah and rabbinic laws emphasize compassion to
animals. For example, "If thou see the ass of your enemy under its
burden, thou shall not pass him by, thou shall surely unload" (Exod.
23:5). We are forbidden to take the mother bird and her young
together. The mother must be sent away before its young are taken
away (Deut. 22:6–7). The Rambam said that we do this because we
want to spare the mother bird the pain of seeing her children taken
away. This compassion to animals is not because they are on the
same level as us but rather because the Torah mandates that we
human beings should take care of animals.

Another important reason to embrace vegetarianism is that
worldwide vegetarianism would reduce world hunger. Grains are fed
to livestock in third-world countries, even though the people there
do not have food to eat. According to Schwartz, "The world's cattle
consume an amount of food equivalent to the calorie requirements
of 8.7 billion people. Livestock in the United States eat ten times the
grain that Americans eat directly." In the report by the Viva Vegie
Society entitled "101 Reasons to Be a Vegetarian," we are told that
it takes an average of twenty-five hundred gallons of water to produce a single pound of meat. In contrast, it takes only twenty-five

gallons of water to produce one pound of wheat. A great many of the natural resources that are used to raise cattle could be devoted to raising grains and vegetables, which would enable us to feed many more people. God created a world where there are more than enough natural resources to feed every person. However, these resources have to be shared.

The Bible begins with man being instructed to eat the fruits of the trees. "And God said, 'Behold I have given you every herb yielding seed that is upon the face of the earth and every tree in which is the fruit of a tree yielding seed. To you it shall be for food'" (Gen. 1:29). Vegetarianism was the original divine vision. God wanted us to eat fruits and vegetables. Some say that our bodies are designed to eat vegetables and not meat. Our teeth, our intestinal tracts, our digestive systems are more compatible with a vegetarian diet. Schwartz makes another interesting point in *Judaism and Vegetarianism,* which is that when people were vegetarians they lived hundreds of years. The life span of people was significantly reduced when meat was consumed.

During the time of Noah, man was given permission to eat animals. "And God blessed Noah and his sons and said to them, 'Every moving thing that lives shall be food for you as the green herb. I have given you everything. Only flesh with its living soul—its blood you shall not eat'" (Gen. 9:1–4). Kabbalah says that meat was permitted to Noah because he was a totally righteous person and he wanted to do animal sacrifices. If people eat meat, they should abide by certain laws and restrictions so that they are mindful of what they are doing.

In earlier times, people were forbidden to eat animals unless they went to the wilderness to trap their prey, be it animal or fowl, which was a dangerous and extremely troublesome undertaking. They had to really want to eat meat to go through the trouble of trapping it. Leviticus 17:13 addresses this point. Concerning this, Jewish sages remarked, "The Torah teaches us proper conduct, that a human being should not eat flesh except after such preparation" (Chullin 84a). Jewish sages did not want people to get into the habit of consuming animals. Furthermore, the Bible says, "If anyone captures by hunting any beast or bird that may be eaten, he must pour out its blood, covering it with earth" (Lev. 17:13). Rav Kook said this is the beginning of moral therapy because to cover the blood is an acknowledgment of having committed a shameful act. Eating meat requires greater consciousness. The Torah tells us not to mix meat and milk so as to make us more sensitive about eating meat. An observant Jew who "keeps kosher" and eats both meat and dairy has one set of dishes, pots and pans, and utensils for consuming meat and another set for consuming dairy. The laws governing keeping kosher are intended to make people mindful when eating meat.

There is a debate in Jewish religious circles as to whether God permitted the consumption of meat as a concession to the lusts and desires of man or as a spiritual practice. Eating meat is seen as a way of elevating the sparks of the animal soul so that the animal will be raised to a higher spiritual level than it would be able to reach on its own. There is *midrash* that says God asked each animal if it would agree to be slaughtered if by doing so it would ascend from the level of an ignorant animal to the level of a God-conscious human being. The animals replied, "It is good."

According to the Talmud and kabbalah, however, only the most righteous people are permitted to eat meat, and they must do so with the proper intent of elevating the soul of the animal as they eat. The sages say, "One who is ignorant of Torah is forbidden to eat meat" (Pesachim 49b). Rabbi Yitzchok Luria, as recollected by Rabbi Hayim Vital in *Sha'as Ha Mitzvos,* stated, "His soul which possesses only a small measure of holiness will become fused with the soul of the animal; unable to rectify and remove the spiritual dross which it encounters, this small measure of holiness will then depart. From this one should understand how a person must be careful not to consume too much meat."

In *Reishit Chochma,* the classical introduction to kabbalah, there is a lengthy discussion that concludes that one should not consume the flesh of any living creature. And in another book, *Shevat Mussar,* Rabbi Eliyahu Ha Kohen of Izmir also stated that meat is only permitted to a perfectly righteous person. A common person is not actually forbidden to eat meat, but it is implied that to refrain from eating meat would be very good for such a person. Unfortunately, most people consume meat without the proper intention.

It is common practice for religious Jews to eat lots of meat during holiday celebrations, believing that doing so adds to the celebrations. Some people maintain it is necessary that a person consume meat to celebrate the Sabbath and the Jewish holidays. According to the Talmud (T.B. Pesachim 109a), since the destruction of the Temple, Jews are not required to eat meat in order to rejoice on sacred occasions. People should eat festive foods that help them celebrate the holidays. I often prepare seaweed or a special bean dip in honor of the Sabbath. It is not necessary to eat meat. Eating meat actually places a heavy burden on the digestive system, resulting as well in sluggishness that might detract from absorbing the spirituality of the holiday. Vegetarian food does not tax the digestive system so much, leaving more energy for learning, singing and talking about spirituality.

I became a lifelong vegetarian during a trip to Israel in 1972. Walking through the old city in Jerusalem, I literally saw a side of beef for the first time. I was horrified. Until then I never really thought much about animals being living creatures that were killed for our benefit and pleasure. I only saw packaged meat. I think that many people do not think about the fact that an animal has been slaughtered when they eat meat. I gave up eating meat for health reasons and also because I did not think that someone should kill animals for me if I would not be able to do so myself.

In the past, people did not consume the amount of meat they do now. For one reason, they could not afford it. Jews would have a little chicken on the Sabbath and the rest of the time they were primarily vegetarian. There were no animal factories. When people lived in small villages and farms, everyone knew the person who slaughtered the animal. He was a religious man. He probably prayed each day and went to *mikvah* to purify himself before slaughtering any animal. Prior to being slaughtered, animals had lived full lives outdoors, eating natural foods. I believe when animals were used for sacrifices in the Holy Temple that this may actually have been a spiritual service to the animals. We cannot compare animal sacrifices to animal consumption today. Even though I am a strict vegetarian, I do not think I would have turned down an opportunity to eat of the animal sacrifice in the Holy Temple.

There is a tendency to ridicule vegetarianism in some religious circles. I experienced this critical attitude firsthand, especially in *yeshiva* in the beginning of my becoming religious. I was even told that it was against Judaism to be a vegetarian. It is often uncomfortable for a vegetarian to eat in the homes of traditionally religious people because they will often tell you that you are not fulfilling the *mitzvah* of the Sabbath by not eating meat. I also suspect that they are embarrassed to eat meat in front of you, as you nibble on salad and overcooked vegetables. I believe that this attitude is wrong and unnecessary. I encourage vegetarians to stand strong and not be intimidated for there is much in the Jewish and kabbalistic tradition to support the vegetarian way of life.

16

THE JEWISH MESSIANIC NEW AGE

When we reflect on the suffering in the world—war, poverty, disease, loneliness, selfishness—we know this is not the way the world should be. It is not what God intended for us. Judaism teaches us not to accept the status quo and never to give up our dreams for a better world. One tenet of Judaism is that we should hope for, work for and actively await a time when war, illness and poverty will end, and peace, well-being and the knowledge of God will reign. This is called "the time of the Messiah." The Jewish Messiah will not only redeem the Jewish people but the whole world. The Rambam stated, "If the Messiah takes time in coming, wait for him—do not give up waiting for him. Do not calculate when he will come. Believe that he will come at the right time." Though the time of the coming of the Messiah has always been unknown, in former days some Jews always had a suitcase packed to be ready to go to Israel at a moment's notice.

It is interesting to note that the Gemara says when we die we will be asked three questions: Were you honest in business? Did you establish times to nurture yourself spiritually? Were you waiting for the Messiah? The waiting for the Messiah is the yearning for a world devoted to truth and unity. For admission into this New Age, a person must want such a world.

Why do we await the coming of the Messiah so enthusiastically? It is prophesied that the physical world as we know it now will slowly be transformed and refined during the days of the Messiah. Earning our livelihood will become easier. We will have more leisure time to devote to spirituality. Harmony will be restored between the body and the soul. We will live longer and not suffer from the host of current ailments. The world will be filled with the desire to come close to God, and only things that bring us close to God will be important. We will clearly see the reality and the presence of God in everything, and this will fill us with great joy and gratitude. Relationships between husband and wife and between children and parents will be harmonious. All religious disputes and bickering will be resolved. Everything will be clear. There will be no war, no hunger, no suffering.

Jews believe that this ideal world will become a reality. Though we cannot actually calculate the exact time of this new era, we are told that it will occur before or during the year 6000 in the Jewish calendar. At the time of the writing of this book we are in the year 5760, which is 1999. The Torah says that God created the world in six days and on the seventh day He rested. The six days of Creation parallel the six millennia of the world as we know it. The seventh day is the Sabbath, the day of rest, which corresponds to the seventh millennia. The transformation of the New Age known as the time of the Messiah will occur over a thousand years. After the completion of this thousand-year period, the world will be in the year 7000. At this time, the world will enjoy the total perfection of the original divine vision. The Divine Soul will shine so brightly into the body that we will live forever.

We are now in the Friday afternoon of the sixth millennia. We have only a few hours (240 years) before the Sabbath begins. If we deserve the Messiah coming earlier than the year 6000, it can happen before that date. Whether we are worthy or not, the Messiah will still appear by the year 6000, because it is Divine Will that this be so. "I, God, will hasten (the Redemption) in its due time" (Isa. 60:22). God gave man free will with the opportunity to participate in the redemption of the world. Jews were dispersed all over the world to both ignite and collect the sparks of Godliness in the nations in the world. If we are not successful in completing this task of bringing the Messiah, God will do it. He will not allow us to suffer endlessly.

Many people consider the current times to be the footsteps, or the birth pangs, of the Messiah. The primary sign is the establishment of the state of Israel after 2,000 years of dispersion. Israel welcomes any Jew who wants to settle in the Holy Land. The ingathering of Jews from Russia, Ethiopia and other countries that had previously restricted their travel is a significant sign of the coming of this New Age. It is also important that Jews all over the world enjoy religious and civil freedom in a way that they have not for thousands of years.

There are many other secular signs. The *Zohar* predicts that there will be an explosion in technology. We live in a time of tremendous breakthroughs in every area of science and technology. New developments are reported every day. Many recent scientific discoveries corroborate kabbalistic teachings and fulfill ancient prophecies. We can now see how the ancient prophecies of long life and healthy children will be fulfilled. For example, scientific breakthroughs in genetic engineering hold the promise of an elimination of birth defects, also making it possible for women in their fifties and sixties to bear children. Even cloning, the possibility of replicating body parts, may hold secrets for increased longevity.

Another sign is the change in the position of woman. The Torah says in Genesis that woman was cursed when Eve tempted Adam to eat from the Tree of Good and Evil: "I will increase your suffering in childbearing, in pain shall you bear children, yet your craving shall be for your husband and he shall rule over you." Kabbalah says in the times of the Messiah, the curse of woman will be lifted. Women will be elevated and resume their higher status. They will not suffer in childbirth. Women will move more and more into leadership roles in both the secular and religious arenas. "A woman will court a man" (Jer. 31:22). We see this happening as well. The change in the status of woman during the times of the Messiah will be reflected in a change in the Jewish marriage ceremony. In traditional wedding ceremonies, the woman circles the man seven times. However, it is said that in the times of the Messiah, the man will circle the woman seven times. The feminine principle will be dominant.

In the days approaching the coming of the Messiah, a greater desire and potential for unity will manifest. We now have at our disposal communication technologies that allow us to make contact instantaneously with people around the world. All this will be helpful to the Messiah. People all over the world will easily be able to see and hear him. We live in a time when there is greater sharing of information and resources among diverse cultures. We are beginning to realize that what happens in one part of the globe affects the whole world. We talk of a global village. We recognize that the economies of nations are interdependent. For example, if Japan's economy collapses, we in the United States are affected. People in the West are becoming easternized and the people in the East are becoming westernized. World travel is accessible for most people.

Most importantly, there is a general awakening of interest in spirituality throughout the world. Books on spirituality enjoy great success worldwide. Synagogues and churches are experiencing a revival and increased attendance. Close to my apartment in New York City is a synagogue, B'nai Jeshurun, which now has three thousand people in attendance at Friday-night services. It is now fashionable and popular to be involved in Judaism in this metropolis. This was not true ten years ago. I think it is also a sign of Messianic times that there is an amazing revival of Christianity in communist countries, such as China and Russia, which restrict religious involvement. Because religious expression is restricted in China, people practice secretly at great personal risk.

Meditation is so mainstream today that it is even accepted as a way to reduce stress, and meditation instruction is considered a payable benefit by some insurance companies. More and more people are raising their consciousness and dedicating themselves to fostering unity in the world. This is also a sign of the New Age. The kabbalists predicted a general revival of interest in kabbalah and that its secrets would be made available. We see this happening as well. Previously unavailable manuscripts on kabbalah have been translated and are now widely available. Even movie stars, such as Madonna, Elizabeth Taylor and Roseanne, study kabbalah and testify in magazines and on television that kabbalah has helped them. I think this is great.

At the same time, the forces of darkness and evil are greater. The collapse of the Soviet Union has made nuclear and biological weaponry more accessible to terrorist groups and governments who support terrorism. Though terrorism is a relatively new international phenomenon, there have been several episodes of terrorism in the United States and there will possibly be more in the future. It is frightening to know that extremists possess such dangerous implements of war. It does not appear that the world is on the brink of peace. There appears to be more nationalism and fighting according to religious affiliations. So many wars are waged in the world today that I have trouble understanding and keeping track of them.

In his book *The Knowing Heart,* the Ramchal, Rabbi Moses Luzzatto, said, "God will allow evil to intensify to its fullest extent, that is, until, but not including the destruction of the universe. . . . Though evil is intensifying, the righteous must abide its oppression—not because this is just, but because the time requires it. . . . In the final outcome, the righteous will receive greater reward than they would have received by virtue of their own merit." It is not known how much evil the world will have to endure before people turn to God. The Lubavitcher Rebbe reassured us that the world will not be destroyed and that no significant change will occur when the Messiah appears. The Jewish people have already paved the way for the Messiah through their suffering during the Holocaust and their increasing good deeds. Many people feel that there will not be any Jewish suffering of such magnitude again. The call of the Lubavitcher Chassidim is "The time for the Messiah is now." I do not believe that community would call for the Messiah if it was going to cause pain and destruction.

Many people are afraid of the Messianic Age, associating it with Armageddon. Christian fundamentalists anticipate the second coming of Jesus and say that it will be preceded by "the battle of Armageddon," during which millions of Jews will be destroyed unless they become Christians. According to a recent report in the *Jewish Week* newspaper of New York, "Jerry Falwell, the founder of the Moral Majority, may be good friends with the Prime Minister of

Israel, but he is espousing an evangelical belief that an anti-Christ figure will soon appear and he will be a Jewish man, and he will wage war against the Jews." This person will usher in a "Tribulation Period," during which the remainder of Jews will be converted to Christianity after destruction of massive proportions. Sounds like a hateful prophecy to me. I wonder why Christians don't plead or pray for Jews to be saved even if they don't convert. That would be a demonstration of Christian mercy. Abraham pleaded with God to save Sodom and Gomorrah.

Christian prophecy appears to be a distortion of Jewish biblical prophecy. Biblical prophecies are also frightening. For example, the prophet Zechariah declares, "There will be a day which will be the Lord's day, the day which the Holy One has appointed for taking vengeance on the idolatrous nations" (Zech. 14:2). The *Zohar* gives this prophecy based on Zechariah: "A star in the East will swallow seven stars in the north, and a flame of black fire will hang toward the north in which two kings will perish. All the nations shall combine against the daughter of Jacob in order to drive her out of the world. . . . All the kings of the world will assemble in the great city of Rome, and the Holy One will shower on them fire and hail and meteoric stones until they are all destroyed. From that time, the Messiah will begin to declare himself, and round him there will be gathered many nations and many hosts from uttermost ends of the earth. . . . The children of Ishmael will at the same time rouse all the peoples of the world to come up to war against Jerusalem, as it is written, for I will gather all nations against Jerusalem to battle." We have already seen the nations of the Arab world rally together unsuccessfully to destroy the state of Israel, and it appears that they may once again be planning another attempt. Zechariah predicts about people who wage war against Jerusalem that "their flesh will rot while they stand on their feet, their eyes will rot in their sockets, and their tongues will rot in their mouths" (Zech. 14:12). Sounds like nuclear war, God forbid. Zechariah says that all remaining will come to worship in Jerusalem: "If any of the nations of the earth does not come up to Jerusalem . . . there will be no rain upon it" (Zech. 14:86).

The *Zohar* continues based on a prophecy from Isaiah: "Happy are those who will be left at the end of the sixth millennium to enter on the Sabbath. . . . And it shall come to pass, that he that is left in Zion, and he that remaineth, in Jerusalem, shall be called holy, even every one that is written unto life in Jerusalem." It would appear from this prophecy that people will die in this last battle.

There are many other frightening biblical predictions, but it is important to note that doomsday prophecies are not carved in stone. People can change the course of history by *teshuvah*. If we think and do good, things will be good. Psalm 91 reminds us to seek the refuge of God in times of trouble: "He who dwells in the shelter of the Supreme One, he will abide. He will save you from the snare trap from destructive pestilence. A thousand will fall at your left side and ten thousand at your right side, but it shall not come near you." Our faith in God is our greatest protection from harm. Most rabbis I know and consulted regarding this chapter believe that the last war, which will be led by the Messiah to vanquish evil, will not be a physical battle but a spiritual and intellectual conflict.

Just as Moses was the Messiah for the Jewish people and performed many miracles that led the Jewish people peacefully out of Egypt, the Messiah to come will fight this last war with words of prayer. Isaiah says, "He will smite the wicked with the rod of his mouth, and with the spirit of his lips he will slay evildoers. . . . On that day, man will cast away his silver gods and his golden gods, that each made for himself to worship" (Isa. 2:20). This refers to the idolatry of wealth and power. People will relinquish the materialism that has defined their lives. If people are attached to things that are not based in truth or Godliness, it may be hard for them to embrace the truth that the Messiah will bring. During the days of the Messiah, the lifestyles of illusion and artifice will become transparent. There will be people who will challenge the Messiah, but they will fail and perish.

Who is the Messiah? Judaism says that he will be a descendant of the House of David. He will be a righteous person born of ordinary parents. At a certain point in his life, he will be anointed with an influx of Godliness that will distinguish him as the Messiah. "Upon the Messiah will descend a spirit of God, a spirit of wisdom and understanding, a spirit of advice and strength, a spirit of knowledge and fear of God. And he shall breathe the fear of God; he will not judge by what he sees nor by what he hears, He will judge righteously" (Isa. 11:2–4).

Other ancient Jewish teachings state that there will be two Messiahs, Messiah ben Joseph and Messiah ben David. There are varying opinions about the connection between these two figures. The Gemara says that Messiah ben Joseph will precede and pave the way for Messiah ben David. One opinion says that Messiah ben Joseph will stand for the non-Jewish world (the assimilated Ten Tribes of Israel) and Messiah ben David for the Jewish world. I wonder this: If Jesus was Messiah ben Joseph as Christians believe him to be, if he does come back as he was in his previous lifetime—as an orthodox Jewish man—how will Jews and Christians respond?

According to Jewish prophecy, the Messiah will be recognized easily as a world leader. Upon seeing his radiance, witnessing his great love and compassion, people will easily be inspired to come to the truth of God. In our present world, where there are few leaders to respect, the Messiah will offer the leadership we are hungry for. Though he will sit in Jerusalem, he will unite the world. Television will allow his message to be heard instantaneously throughout the world.

Though the term "Messiah" refers to an actual person, Judaism believes that the Messiah is within the consciousness of every person. We all carry the sparks of Messiah within us. Though we await a person who will embody this consciousness and unite the world, we each have to develop this consciousness ourselves. In our own small ways, in acts of love and kindness, we can share redemptive messianic moments and see sparks of the Messiah within each other. Any devoted follower of a rebbe sees this potential of the Messiah in his teacher. At certain times when I was with Reb Shlomo Carlebach, I was so blissful that I said to myself, "This is Gan Eden, this is paradise. How could I want more?" When the Tzemach Tzedek, the third Lubavitcher Rebbe, lived, his followers also felt that they had received everything that a person could receive from the Messiah. They asked, "What will the Messiah achieve? We have the revelation now." It is said that in each generation there is a potential Messiah and that the vision of the Messiah was not realized because the people were not ready for the revelation.

In New Age circles, this story of the one-hundredth monkey is told to explain how the New Age will emerge: On a tropical island, one monkey discovered that he could wash a banana in the ocean before eating it. Other monkeys on the island saw what this monkey had done, and they began to wash their bananas before eating them. When a critical mass of 100 monkeys began to wash their bananas, the researchers were astonished to notice that monkeys on other islands also simultaneously began to wash their bananas. Even though the monkeys on the other islands had no way of communicating, they influenced each other. Thus, when a sufficient number of people have developed a consciousness of spiritual unity, the rest of mankind will be uplifted.

It is significant that billions of Christians are also waiting for the Messiah, even if with a different understanding than Jews have. The Rambam stated that one of the benefits of Christianity is that it taught the people of the world about the concept of God and the Messiah and that the world needs to be on a higher level of faith before the Messiah actually comes. The problem that Jews have with Christianity, according to the Rambam, is not that Jesus was considered the Messiah but that he was considered God. Jesus was rejected as the Messiah by the Jewish people because he did not redeem them or bring lasting peace to the world. He did not fulfill the mandate of the Messiah as predicted in the ancient prophecies. No person has, so far, though there have been many Jews who were considered the Messiah for brief periods of time, including one person in our generation. The Lubavitcher Rebbe, Rabbi Menachem Mendel Schneerson, was hailed as the Messiah by his followers up to and even after his death in 1994.

What prevents the Messiah from coming or from being actualized? The Chofetz Chayim, a most respected scholar of the early twentieth century, said that the main impediment is senseless hatred. The divisiveness among the Jewish people hinders the coming of the Messiah. Jews must stop bickering and love each other. What will bring the Messiah? Love, performing good deeds, providing charity and doing God's Will.

I believe that meditation is important because it provides a taste of the Messiah. Through meditation we open to the consciousness of the Messiah within ourselves. It is also important to talk about the coming of the Messiah and instill in people a hope that life will be better. It is not a false hope. It is a hope that is grounded in the ancient prophecies.

CONCLUSION

The power and durability of Judaism rest on its capacity to be dynamic and relevant to every time, yet also to have constancy and permeability. Since its beginning in ancient times, Judaism has undergone several major and minor paradigm shifts. The external forms of Judaism may vary from time to time, but the essential, inner and mystical teachings of Judaism remain intact and vibrant. There have been many New Age periods of time in Jewish history.

According to many, the world is currently beginning a major paradigm shift, which in New Age astrology is called the "Age of Aquarius" and in Jewish terminology is called the "Age of Moshiach." In his book *Paradigm Shift,* Rabbi Zalman Schachter-Shalomi identified this period as corresponding to the world of *Atzilut,* the highest spiritual world, a place of unity. In *Atzilut,* God and the world are unified.

The Talmud says that the story of Creation recorded in the Bible reveals the plan for the world. Each day of Creation refers to a different 1,000-year period. The first 2,000 years are *Tohu,* chaos. The next 2,000 years are Torah, the time of divine revelation. The final 2,000 years are the time of preparation for the Messianic era. The great Sabbath, the time of our perfection, corresponds to the seventh day. We are currently in late Friday afternoon. According to the Jewish calendar, the year 5760 corresponds to 1999 to 2000.

The last major paradigm shift occurred 2,000 years ago, which was, interestingly enough, around the time of Jesus. Around 600 B.C.E., the great Jewish prophets Isaiah, Ezekiel and Jeremiah tried to prepare the people for the upcoming major changes of the paradigm shift they would undergo. Previous to that time, Judaism had been centered around the Holy Temple in Jerusalem. God dwelled like a king in Jerusalem. When the Holy Temple was destroyed, many Jews perished. In their desire to preserve the Jewish transmission as authentically as possible, the rabbis extended Judaism to fit the needs of the Jewish people in exile. The rabbis developed the prayer book to keep the Jewish people unified in the way that the Temple did. Prayer replaced Temple sacrifices. The rabbis introduced the practice of lighting Sabbath candles and reciting blessings over the meal to replace Temple worship. The Sabbath table where a person eats and says blessings was intended to be envisioned as the altar in the Holy Temple. In this way, the Divine Presence, the *Shechinah,* which was formerly stationary in the Holy Temple, would now travel in exile with the people. God, no longer confined to one space, could be found wherever Jewish rabbinic law was followed. The new concept of holiness in time actually expanded the former concept of holiness confined to one space. Over time, subject to the challenges of persecution and assimilation, many Jews moved away from rabbinic Judaism. Whenever there was a great need or too much assimilation among the Jewish people, a great and holy Jewish soul would appear—such as Rabbi Yitzchok Luria, the Baal Shem Tov, Rabbi Moses Luzzatto and many others—to serve as divine emissaries to bring Jews back to God and usher in a period of renewal and revival of Judaism.

Like the destruction of the Holy Temple, which ushered in a new paradigm, I believe that the newest spiritual paradigm has been ushered in by another time of destruction, the Holocaust, which prepared the ground for the establishment of the state of Israel after 2,000 years. The establishment of Israel is extremely significant to the Jewish people, to millions of Christians and to Moslems as well. The conquest of Jerusalem in 1967 by Israel was an additional signpost for many of the New Age. Before our very eyes, we are witnessing the unfolding of the New Age. It is not yet clear what the full impact and implications of the establishment of Israel will be for the Jewish people and for the world in general, and the Jewish people are very divided as to what the identity of Israel should be. Should Israel be a religious state, a return to days of old, with a Holy Temple and animal sacrifices? Should Israel be a liberal, progressive and democratic state? Israel appears to be, as in days of old, divided into two kingdoms. Tensions are mounting. The painful, divisive and ironic contradictions of Jewish life in Israel scream out the need for New Age Judaism. Only the most inner and deepest revelation of Godliness will bring unity to the Jewish people.

"Behold, days are coming," speaks God through the prophet Jeremiah, "when I will make a new covenant with the House of Israel and the House of Judah, not like the covenant that I made with their ancestors, when I redeemed them from Egypt, which they violated. . . . This is the covenant . . . I will place My Torah within them and inscribe it upon their hearts" (Jer. 31:30–32). Many of us are eagerly awaiting this new covenant, a Judaism for the New Age. We are open to receiving the Torah of the heart. We yearn to open our hearts to the unity of God and experience our essential oneness with other people.

Many people, like myself, are tired of Jewish politics being divided into little Jewish sects, separated from each other and separated from other groups of people. Today most Jews no longer live or want to live in Jewish ghettos, like Jews did for thousands of years. We want to be Jews radiating the universal, loving message of Judaism and bringing forth a new world order of peace. We, this baby-boom generation, the *gilgul* of the Shoah, the reincarnated souls of those who perished in the Holocaust, have had enough of senseless bickering. We are particularly ready for the peace and unity of a New Age. As Rabbi Shlomo Carlebach sang, "The whole world is waiting to sing the song of *Shabbos*." The whole world needs to experience the oneness of God, particularly God's holy city, Jerusalem, whose name means "City of Peace."

When I first went to Israel as a religious person in the early 1980s, I was greatly pained by the divisiveness I witnessed in the Jewish community. While I was growing up, my family had belonged to orthodox, conservative and reform synagogues simultaneously. It did not seem odd to me at the time. One of the most beautiful teachings I received from my father of blessed memory was that a Jew should be comfortable in any synagogue where Jews are gathered to pray. As an adult I attended the synagogue of Reb Shlomo Carlebach, where all kinds of Jews prayed together, from men wearing black coats and women wearing wigs and hats to men and women in T-shirts and jeans. Reb Shlomo radiated unconditional love and acceptance to everyone. This was very important to me.

Unconditional love is what is needed to usher in a New Age. If the Jewish people could love each other unconditionally regardless of differences in their religious practices, they would truly be a light to the nations of the world as the biblical prophecy states. Just because people are different from us does not mean that we should withhold our love and respect for them. The differences among people are actually minor in comparison to what we share as human beings. Unconditional love must apply to all people, not just Jews. The New Age will be upon us when we human beings really understand that God is not the property of any specific group of people. When we really grasp the words of the *Shema* that state that God is one, we will see God reflected within everyone, and we will be filled with a great love of God. When we allow our hearts to be truly opened, we will be deeply in love with every person and realize that we always were. This will be the New Age.

I believe that meditation is the fastest and most direct way to experience unconditional love for oneself and for others. We live in an auspicious time of great spiritual influx. In the dawning of this New Age, we do not have to do very much to have a spiritual experience. God's Light is shining brightly today, yet we do need to be receptive. Kabbalah means "to receive," and we need only to open to receive by first experiencing ourselves and viewing everything as a vessel for God's Light. To plug into this experience of God's Light, we need to meditate and pray that we be brought close to God. Then we have to breathe deeply, let go of our concepts, open to be a vessel and allow God to enter.

I encourage everyone, Jew and non-Jew alike, who is so inspired to dive into the waters of Torah. There are wonderful treasures you will find within yourself. Your experience of God, of Judaism, will be better and grow deeper with time and dedication on your part. I also have to caution you, as with any serious spiritual path, that the Jewish path is not easy. Always remember Rabbi Nachman of Breslov for the following words: "Never give up!" There will be many challenges along the way, and at times you may feel discouraged. You may wonder if this is the train you want to ride into eternity. Your faith and commitment will be challenged, but you will grow.

Though God is everywhere, I warn you that it may be hard to experience God, especially in the synagogue. Synagogues are typically noisy. People come to socialize as well as pray. Prayers are often said routinely, from a sense of obligation. Unfortunately, there is little expectation for many of having a spiritual experience in synagogue. It is tragic that Jews as a whole have not learned how to prepare themselves for prayer or how to pray in a meditative way with feeling and devotion. We can actually experience something wonderful in prayer. If we are the same after prayer, as before, then we didn't really pray.

Upon arriving in a town, the Baal Shem Tov walked into its synagogue and left immediately. When he was asked why he left so abruptly, he replied, "The synagogue is too full of prayers." He was asked, "Shouldn't a synagogue be filled with prayers?" The Baal Shem Tov responded, "No. Heartfelt prayers ascend to God. Prayers said without true feeling remain."

Remember that the synagogue is not the only place for a divine encounter. God is everywhere. The Peasantzer Rebbe, the rebbe of the Warsaw ghetto gave us the following advice, which may be helpful to many people: "If your faith in God is wavering, you need to transcend your mind and your problems for a few minutes." He recommended that we go to the forest to meditate: "See yourself as a pure creature among God's creatures, like the sun and moon, and sing before God to reveal and fill the world with Divine goodness. Proclaim to the other creatures and to the world that God is the Master. As you do this you will see if your soul doesn't break out in glory to meet your Maker and a supernal fire will burn in you which will only be quenched by tears."

We each must find our own connection to God in our own unique way, and it is to God alone that we must make an accounting. We pray to the God of Abraham, Isaac and Jacob. Each of them found his own connection to God, as we must also do for ourselves. I have heard of many people who abandon a Jewish connection because of their experiences with rabbis or with religious people. To do so is unfortunate and misguided. It is important that we see all the obstacles we encounter in our Jewish journey, and in our life in general, as spiritual tests and opportunities to grow. It is a Jewish practice that when people want to convert to Judaism, they are discouraged and asked to determine the extent of their desire. Even for people born into the Jewish faith, there will be internal and external obstacles and barriers, which they will have to overcome to prove their commitment to enter into the true Light of God. Reb Nachman said that the extent of the barrier is often an indication of the gift that is on the other side. It is also important to remember that God will not put up a barrier that is too great for you to overcome. This is a path of love and compassion.

Sometime in your spiritual journey, you may wonder, "Why does God not shine His light and love directly to me, making Himself so irresistible that not only am I totally sure that He exists, but I cannot help love Him and do His will? Why is it so hard?" It occurred to me that it is because God wants us to love Him that He sometimes conceals His light and goodness from us. If God would shine His light directly to us, revealing His goodness, we would automatically love Him because He is good to us. His goodness would overwhelm us. By concealing Himself, He tests us. This test refines us. He wants to see if we really love Him. He plays hide and seek. Sometimes God even flirts with us, encouraging us to seek Him. Sometimes we see Him, we feel Him directly, and other times He is hidden and we wonder where He is. When we continually look for him hidden in our lives and even search for Him in the dark places of our lives, He may give us a glimpse of Himself. When we yearn for Him, whether we are happy, whether or not good things are happening to us, when we never forget Him, and when He knows that we really love Him, then He reveals Himself to us. If God were totally revealed, we would not have the opportunity to pursue Him and demonstrate our love for Him. What need would there be for faith if there were no concealment?

In your journey in Judaism, you will hear many things about what Judaism is. Some might not be true, and others you will be unready to accept. I recall that there were things I heard in the early days of my religiousness that I could not accept and that I was actually appalled by, but in time I grew to understand and realize the beauty and depth of the very ideas about which I was so resistant. On our spiritual journey, timing—how ready and how open we are to God's Light—is so important. Even more important is connecting with the teachers who hold the keys to opening our souls. There are many wonderful teachers throughout the Jewish world. Do not deprive yourself. Do not feel that you have to be orthodox to learn from someone who is orthodox. There are also wonderful spiritual teachers in the non-orthodox world. Go to people and places where there is spiritual light and joy. Search out the teachers who will spark your soul and open your heart. Keep looking and praying that you find the right teachers. The entire Jewish world is open to you. Don't be shy. If a teacher puts you or others down, he is not for you. Meanwhile, read spiritual books. Do not be afraid to read the amazing classics, such as *Duties of the Heart, The Way of God, The Knowing Heart, Tanya.* These works allow you to experience yourself in the presence of very great spiritual beings. Most importantly, pray to find a living rebbe or *tzaddik.* If you attach yourself to such a person, you will receive much more spiritually than what you would have merited on your own. It is a great spiritual gift to have a rebbe.

Judaism is undergoing an exciting renaissance today. The House of Israel is once again being rebuilt. There is increasing vitality in all branches of Judaism. There is much more Jewish learning being offered than ever before. Synagogue services in the Jewish community are more joyful than when I was growing up. I think that is in part because many more synagogues are incorporating the melodies of my rebbe and teacher of blessed memory, Reb Shlomo Carlebach. Religious organizations are slowly responding to the pressure put upon them to bring forth mystical teachings. I have seen several orthodox Jewish organizations begin to offer classes in kabbalah when only last year they spoke out vehemently against the study of kabbalah. Even rabbis in the Reform movement of Judaism are teaching kabbalah.

I encourage each of you to make a commitment to your spiritual growth. Anyone who achieves anything spiritually does so through great devotion. This is true for our greatest teachers. They were the greatest because they worked the hardest. It may be hard to find the right synagogue or the right community, yet you can still strive to be the best possible person you can be. This is your life purpose: to develop the unique divine imprint that is within you. No one can do it for you. Do not compare yourself with anyone. We are always growing from where we are and the sky is the limit. God is infinite and the path to God is also infinite.

GLOSSARY

Adam Kadmon	primordial man; the world that still is part of Ain Sof; the first world God revealed
Adam	the first human being
Adonoy	Lord, as in *Adonoy Eloheinu,* "the Lord Your God"
Ain Sof	the kabbalistic name for God, "without limit"
Alter Rebbe	the first rebbe of Lubavitch
Assiyah	the fourth world, the world of "making," of action
Atzilut	the first world, "nearness"
Beriyah	the second world, "something from nothing," the "Universe of the Throne"
bikur cholim	the *mitzvah* of visiting the sick
Binah	the third *sephira,* understanding
bittul	nothingness, self-nullification
Chassid, Chassidim (pl.)	a person who follows the path of a

	rebbe or is meticulous in religious observance
Chassidus	the study of Chassidism
chaya	soul energy
chayot	a type of angel
Chochmah	the second *sephira,* the beginning of consciousness
Daat	knowledge
daven	to pray
Devekut	"cleaving to God"
dybbuk	soul of another that invades a person as an alien force intermittently or continually
Ehyeh Asher Ehyeh	one of God's names, "I will be what I will be"
Elohim	name of God associated with Creation
Etz Hayim	*Tree of Life,* the teachings of Rabbi Yitzchok Luria
Gemara	compilation of rabbinic discussions to elucidate the Mishnah
Gevurah	the fifth sephira, strength
gilgul	reincarnation
hait	sin
Hashem	the name used by religious Jews for God, "the Name"
Hesed	the fourth *sephira,* lovingkindness or abundance

Hod	the eighth *sephira,* humility, splendor
hovey	to be
ibur	partial reincarnation of righteous person in a living person
Kabbalah	Jewish mystical tradition
Kaddish	prayer for the deceased
kavanna, kavannot (pl.)	intention, concentration, contemplations, meditations
keter	the first *sephira,* the Crown
Kiddush	sanctification of wine
klippot	shells, impurity
Lech Lecha	third portion of the Torah
loshon hara	evil gossip, evil speech
Makom	the "Place of the World"
malach, malachim (pl.)	angel, messenger
mashpiya	spiritual guide and transmitter
mazel	luck
merkava	chariot for the Divine Presence
middot	personal qualities
midrash	a story in the Jewish oral tradition, a legend
mikvah	ritual bath
minyan	quorum of ten required for prayer
Mishkon	portable ark

Mishnah	commentary of rabbis elucidating the Five Books of Moses
mitzraim	Egypt, place of constraint
mitzvah, mitzvot (pl.)	commandment
nefesh	the level of soul most associated with the body
neshama	the witness-consciousness level of soul, soul
Netzach	the seventh *sephira*, victory, endurance
niggun	song without words
ophanim	types of angels
Or Ain Sof	Limitless Light
pelaigish	concubine
rav	rabbi
rebbe	spiritual teacher
Reishit Chochma	a kabbalistic text
ruach	level of soul connected to the heart
Sefer Yetzirah	ancient text of Jewish meditation
sephira, sephirot (pl.)	divine emanations
Shabbat	Sabbath
Shabbos	Sabbath
Shechinah	Divine Presence
shedim	demons

Shema	a short prayer said several times a day, basic affirmation of Judaism: "Hear, O Israel, the Lord your God, the Lord is One," *"Shema Yisrael, Adonoy Eloheynu, Adonoy Echod"*
shidduch	a match for marriage
Shoah	Holocaust
tahor	open to the life force, pure
tallis	prayer shawl
Talmud	Mishnah and Gemara
tameh	impure; closed; cut off from the life force
tefillin	leather prayer scrolls worn on head and left arm
teshuvah	repentance
Tiferet	the sixth *sephira,* beauty, compassion, harmony
tikvah	hope
Torah	God's revelation in the Five Books of Moses
Tosafos	later commentary on Torah, Gemara and Mishnah
tzaddik, tzaddikim (pl.)	righteous person
tzimtzum	contraction
yehida	the highest level of soul that is unified with God

yeshiva	place of Jewish spiritual learning
Yesod	the ninth *sephira,* associated with bonding, foundation
yetzer hara	an evil inclination
yetzer tov	a good inclination
Yetzirah	the third world, "to form"
YHVH	the most familiar name of God, the tetragrammaton
Yisrael	Israel, from the Hebrew *Yeshar* and *El,* "straight to God"
Zer Anpin	the "Small Face" or the "Son," the emotional *sephirot* energies
Zohar	a primary and ancient text of Jewish mysticism

ABOUT THE AUTHOR

Melinda Ribner, C.S.W. and psychotherapist, is the director and founder of the Jewish Meditation Circle and Beit Miriam. She has taught Jewish meditation for over sixteen years at synagogues of all affiliations in the United States and Canada and at such respected New Age centers as Elat Chayyim in Accord, New York, Kripalu Center for Yoga and Health in Lenox, Massachusetts, Interface in Boston and The Open Center in New York. She also has taught at such Jewish academic institutions as Academy for Jewish Religion, Hebrew Union College and the Jewish Theological Seminary, and at such Jewish community organizations as Lubavitch Women's Organizations, Hadassah, the National Council of Jewish Women and United Jewish Appeal. She frequently uses meditation as a treatment modality in her private practice as a psychotherapist.

Melinda, also known as Mindy, received a nonrabbinical ordination to teach Jewish meditation from the legendary Rabbi Shlomo Carlebach. The ordination was witnessed and signed by Rabbi Yidel Stein and Rabbi Dr. Seymour Appelbaum, both Orthodox rabbis. She is the author of *Everyday Kabbalah: A Practical Guide for Jewish Meditation, Healing, and Personal Growth* and *The Gift of a New Beginning*.

Individuals interested in meditation tapes, studying privately with Ms. Ribner, participating in meditation retreats or attending classes of the Jewish Meditation Circle at Beit Miriam may contact her directly at 212-799-1335 or *Ribner@email.msn.com*. She is currently working on a Web site. She is available for lectures or workshops for community organizations.

More of the Inspiration You've Been Waiting For

Chicken Soup for the Writer's Soul

Whether you're a beginning writer, seasoned pro or a writer at heart, the stories of purpose, passion, endurance and success contained in this volume will inform, entertain, uplift and inspire you.

Code #7699 • Quality Paperback • $12.95

Chicken Soup for the Golden Soul

Celebrating the myriad joys of living and the wisdom that comes from having lived, this collection offers loving insights and wisdom—all centering on the prime of life.

Code #7257
Quality Paperback • $12.95

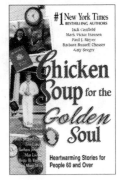

Chicken Soup for the Teenage Soul III

The third volume for teens is here, offering more stories on love, friendship, family, tough stuff, growing up, kindness, learning lessons and making a difference.

Code #7613
Quality Paperback • $12.95

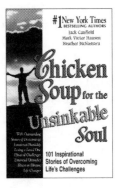

Chicken Soup for the Unsinkable Soul

This book emphasizes triumph in the face of overwhelming odds. A timeless testament to the indomitable human spirit, this collection is sure to encourage, support, comfort and, most of all, inspire you for years to come.

Code #6986 • Quality Paperback • $12.95

The Power to Heal

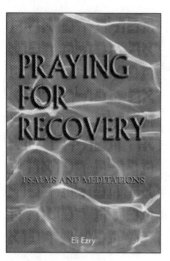

Praying for Recovery

This book is dedicated to helping all recovery addicts find a deeper a connection with their Higher Power. The author presents his own experience in overcoming his skepticism about a personal God and learning to pray for recovery with an open heart.

Code #7885 • Quality Paperback • $7.95

Healing Leaves

Many of us, faced with the ups and downs of everyday life, are searching for the inner strength and confidence to renew our lives in a positive and meaningful way. Reb Noson's letters, based on the understanding and love he learned from the great chassidic master, Rebbe Nachman of Breslov, show how each of us can find that strength.

Code #7656 • Quality Paperback • $7.95

Fiction from Simcha Press

Esther

This is a remarkable love story that spans thirty years from Max and Esther's first meeting in London and her move to Jerusalem where Judaism becomes part of her life. A literary prize brings her back into Max's orbit while her commitment to Israel divides them again. It is finally during an accidental meeting in the middle of war-torn Lebanon that they rediscover the complexities of emotion that bind a man to a woman.

Code #8229 • Quality Paperback • $9.95

The Promise of God

What if the word of God emerged from the drug-ridden cities of South America? What if the world's most prominent media mogul took up the cause for world peace? What if powerful forces in the universe seemed to be drawing toward an unavoid-able and monumental collision? This exciting adventure will take you around the world and keep you on the edge of your seat as the set-up for final eradication of anti-Semitism.

Code #7443 • Quality Paperback • $9.95

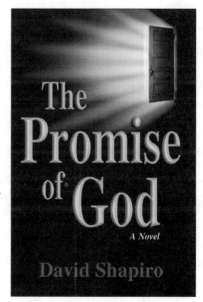

He's Just a Click Away

thelordismyshepherd.com

"You are about to experience the Internet in a way that is both very new and very old, as a modern-day sacred text, a source of spiritual inspiration and fulfillment."

"Join me as we travel through a world that transcends time and space, built upon the elements of Creation. Using the tools of ancient wisdom, modern technology and plain old gut instinct, we are ready to begin an adventure that our grandparents could not have imagined, a pilgrimage without dust. Who knows where we will end up?"

Code #8210
Quality Paperback • $10.95

Joshua Hammerman

thelordismyshepherd.com opens a new and necessary dialogue on the soul of cyberspace. It will change the way you think about your computer, about God, about the future and about the interconnected destiny of humanity in this ever-shrinking world. The author, a noted rabbi and journalist, alternates between analytic and experiential approaches to the subject, escorting you on a multi-dimensional quest for spiritual and intellectual growth.